UNDERGROUND MANUAL FOR SPIRITUAL SURVIVAL

UNDERGROUND MANUAL FOR SPIRITUAL SURVIVAL

LARRY NEAGLE

MOODY PRESS
CHICAGO

© 1986 by
LARRY E. NEAGLE

All rights reserved. No part of this book may be reproduced in any form without permission in writing from the publisher, except in the case of brief quotations embodied in critical articles or reviews.

All Scripture quotations, unless otherwise noted, are from the *New American Standard Bible*, © 1960, 1962, 1963, 1968, 1971, 1972, 1973, 1975, and 1977 by The Lockman Foundation, and are used by permission.

Library of Congress Cataloging-in-Publication Data

Neagle, Larry E., 1949-
    Underground manual for spiritual survival.

    1. Christian life—1960-   I. Title.
BV4501.2.N36   1986   248.4   85-28403
ISBN 0-8024-9052-2 (pbk.)

1 2 3 4 5 6 Printing/ AZ /Year 90 89 88 87 86

Printed in the United States of America

This book is for Paige, Tara, and Joshua, my children, and for Rusty Martin, my friend

ACKNOWLEDGEMENTS

Several years ago I taught a Sunday school class of seminary students. One day a member said, "I feel like I'm dying spiritually, and I don't know what to do." One after another the rest of the class admitted they felt the same way. We spent the next six weeks trying to discover both causes and cures.

From those vulnerable men and women this book was born.

I acknowledge them. Even more I honor them—for teaching the teacher and loving the unlovely.

I would like to acknowledge several others as well. First, Dean Merrill, whose little book *Another Chance: How God Overrides Our Big Mistakes* fell into my hands at approximately the same time. I have never met Dean, and he will never know how much his book has helped me.

Second, Jill Wilson, my editor. She is both patient and caring.

And finally my wife, Deborah. She labored with me, ran constant interference, and endured family times without me. Without her this book would not be.

God bless you all.

CONTENTS

CHAPTER		PAGE
1.	In the Beginning	9
2.	How to Survive a Torpedo Strike	13
3.	No One Bats 1,000	25
4.	Guilt—Friend or Foe	33
5.	What Do I Do with the Memories?	43
6.	A Time to Speak	53
7.	A Time to Listen	63
8.	Cultivating Faithfulness	71
9.	Comforting with the Comfort We've Received	81
10.	Burning Bright but Not Out	91
11.	Going On	101

1
IN THE BEGINNING

God, are you really interested in me?
I feel so empty,
    frustrated,
        and lonely.
I know my life is displeasing to you, but I don't know what to
    do about it.
I thought I would succeed. Instead I've failed.
I thought I had life by the horns. Instead it has me.
I thought sin was defeated, but it seems to be my master.
I don't know how to get from where I am to where I ought to be.
I've slipped and fallen, Lord. And I don't know how much longer
    I can tread water.
If my spiritual ability was swimming ability, I'd be in over my head
    and going down for the third time.
If it was oil in my car, I'd be four quarts low. And my
    car only holds five.
If it was summer heat, I'd be lost in a starless December midnight.
I've tried prayer, but the silence is so hard to interpret.
I've tried reading the Bible, but somehow the words
    don't make sense.
The few friends I've worked up the courage to talk to either didn't
    understand, or didn't care, or didn't know what to say.
Help, Lord.
You pulled Peter out of the water. Pull me.

Life's Lemons

Sound familiar?

Perhaps you haven't used exactly those words before, but the feeling was there—the pain, the defeat. Your dreams were crushed, your self-confidence vaporized, and your hopes for the future annihilated.

Life somehow handed you a lemon. And making lemonade was beyond your ability.

Books abound on the different lemons of life—death and divorce, stress and depression, parents and children. But what about you? How about your own lemon in life? It may not fit someone else's pattern.

Some of the lemons in life are big—tragic mistakes like adultery, theft, illegitimacy, drugs, alcohol, and willful rebellion against that which is right and good. Some come in the tears of separation, birth defects, illness, accidents, paralysis.

Some of the lemons in life are small. Some are simply bad decisions. Oh, they looked right at the time, but looking back they were unmistakably wrong. Financial choices made out of season. Too much credit used up too soon with no way to pay it back. Accepting the wrong job. Staying at it too long. Leaving it too soon. Rashness in marriage. Too many children too soon, or none too late. Quitting school and limiting your potential. Staying too long because it's a warm place to hide. Choosing to live too close to interfering parents or too far away from loving ones.

The size of the lemon has little to do with the amount of pain. Someone once quipped that germs have killed more people than dinosaurs.

Some of the lemons in life come through no fault of our own but through the actions and decisions of others. A drunken driver unable to control his car. Screeching tires. A bereaved parent. Or an empty father, tired of living as he does. One day he walks out and is never seen again.

When I was eight I wanted to be saved. The pastor was unsure I understood, so he counseled that I wait. A year later I approached him with the same desire. This time he thought I understood. A week after my baptism a friend of my mom's stopped me.

"I guess you know you aren't really saved and can't be," she said. "God doesn't give people second chances." Then she misquoted Hebrews 6:4-6 to say that having once been confronted by Christ's claims on my life and not having acted upon them, it was impossible to renew me to repentance.

She was an adult; I was nine. I believed her.

What about you? What about your lemons in life? How can you—with all the limitations you know so well—survive spiritually?

How to Tread Water

How to tread water. That's what this book is designed to teach.

There are a number of books around offering advanced swimming lessons. Many of them are good and ought to be read. But this book focuses on a more immediate need. Long distance swimming, the advantages of different strokes, and so on, are all excellent in their place. But if you can't tread water, you won't make it in the deep end. Think of this book, then, as a short seminar in basic water skills.

That doesn't mean this book is only for new Christians. The lemons in life aren't limited to only the physically or spiritually young or immature. They are disinterested in distinctions. They clobber whom they can, when they can, leaving their victims wounded, bewildered, and bleeding.

In such moments all of us—old and young, mature and immature—need some basic skills to cling to. In the chapters that follow we'll look at nine such skills:

1. Handling undeserved suffering
2. What to do with failure
3. Dealing with guilt
4. Overcoming painful memories
5. Taking it to God, without excuse or concealment
6. Learning to hear God's voice
7. Cultivating faithfulness
8. Comforting others as we've been comforted
9. Burning bright but not out

The Buddy System

When I was a boy taking swimming lessons, the instructor encouraged us never to swim alone. He called it the buddy system. That's what this book is—a buddy system. It won't be a large class but one-on-one, you and me.

You'll find that this is a personal journey. I've intentionally put a lot of my experiences in it, for I struggle too.

And the flow won't be all one way—me to you. Respond. Write and tell me what you think. My address is:

>Larry E. Neagle
>4440 Lubbock Avenue
>Fort Worth, TX 76115

2

HOW TO SURVIVE A TORPEDO STRIKE

Late night war movies tell the story well. An enemy submarine cruises underwater, unseen and unsuspected, stalking the good guys. Carefully the captain lines up his target. He fires. One of the good guys sees the torpedo's wash. But it's too late. The torpedo hits dead center. Soon only an oily patch of debris and a handful of survivors in a lifeboat remain.

Unfortunately life sometimes deals the same to us. All looks well. We steam ahead in a good ship on a smooth ocean. We rejoice in the thought that if things don't get better, neither will they get worse.

Then reality shatters the illusion. Torpedo wash to the starboard. We're under attack.

We knew the enemy was out there somewhere. But we never expected him to find and sink us. We thought he'd hit other ships—those on the edges of the convoy. We expected others—not us. We were prepared for the thought but not the reality.

Now it's too late. We've been hit midship. Much of our

hope, many of our dreams, sink with our ship. And we may not make it through the sharks to the lifeboat.

The Torpedos of Life

In the water, survival is the only question—how to get from here to there without drowning or being eaten by sharks.

We've all been torpedoed in life. We've all been confronted by tragic happenings that come through no fault of our own. A special friend abruptly dies. An untimely lay-off leaves us without income and with little hope for new employment. A home or livelihood lies in ashes, destroyed by what insurance agents call "an act of God." Injury raises its ugly head. A heartbreaking illness swaggers in. Or we find ourselves locked into a devouring situation we can neither control nor escape.

One of the biggest problems in spiritual survival is how to handle unexpected and undeserved suffering.

It's not a new problem. Job faced it. And so did the prophet Jeremiah. Listen to what that prophet had to say:

I am the man who has seen affliction
Because of the rod of His wrath.
He has driven me and made me walk
In darkness and not in light.
Surely against me He has turned His hand
Repeatedly all the day.
He has caused my flesh and my skin to waste away,
He has broken my bones.
He has besieged and encompassed me with bitterness and hardship.
In dark places He has made me dwell,
Like those who have long been dead.
He has walled me in so that I cannot go out;
He has made my chain heavy.
Even when I cry out and call for help,
He shuts out my prayer.
He has blocked my ways with hewn stone;
He has made my paths crooked.
He is to me like a bear lying in wait,
Like a lion in secret places.
He has turned aside my ways and torn me to pieces;
He mas made me desolate.
He bent His bow
And set me as a target for the arrow.
He made the arrows of His quiver
To enter into my inward parts.
I have become a laughingstock to all my people,

Their mocking song all the day.
He has filled me with bitterness,
He has made me drunk with wormwood.
And He has broken my teeth with gravel;
He has made me cower in the dust.
And my soul has been rejected from peace;
I have forgotten happiness.
So I say, "My strength has perished,
And so has my hope from the Lord."

(Lamentations 3:1-18)

WHY?

Why is this happening to me? That's the first question we usually ask in such moments. And we often follow with *What did I do to deserve this?* Both are pointless questions.

Why do we want to know why? Somehow it's comforting for there to be reasons. It fulfills a fundamental need for structure, security, and justice. We want a universe where all the *whys* are alphabetically arranged for quick consultation, study, and understanding. And all the *whats* are itemized as on a bill. Then when disaster strikes, we can demand a reason. Like Job, we can call for an accounting:

> Have I sinned? What have I done to Thee,
> O watcher of men?
> Why hast Thou set me as Thy target,
> So that I am a burden to myself?
>
> (Job 7:20)

> How many are my iniquities and sins?
> Make known to me my rebellion and my sin.
> Why dost Thou hide Thy face,
> And consider me Thine enemy?
>
> (Job 13:23-24)

But Job wasn't told why.

God didn't answer question one. He didn't even attempt to explain. He just revealed Himself, showed Job the error of his thinking, and loved him into new wholeness. (See Job 38-42.)

"Why is this happening to me?" We could just as easily ask, "Why should this not happen to me? What have I done to be exempt?"

NO SPECIAL PROTECTION

Someone has said that the dogma of false religion is "Fear not; trust in God, and He will see that none of the things you fear happen to you." But the truth of real belief is: "Fear not; the things you fear may well happen, but they are nothing to be afraid of."

As God's children, we have presupposed that He has granted us some special protection from the bad things in life—even as the overzealous among us try to give our children special protection. We assume that He has walled us off from everything that causes pain, heartache, and despair. He loves us, the thought goes. Surely He doesn't want us to hurt.

Or, if pain and suffering should come, we assume that He must have some extra special blessing in mind to offset the anguish involved.

Unfortunately both the Bible and everyday life show that God doesn't work that way. In Jesus' parable, Lazarus was one of God's own. Yet he was poor, a beggar, covered with sores. But when the end came it was he who was gathered to Abraham's bosom and not the rich man who had it easy (Luke 16:19-31).

Abraham and Sarah spent the span of their reproductive life childless. And they did it in a time when childlessness was a cause for derision and scorn. Then when the promise came, how easy would it have been to have considered it a little too late? Small wonder Sarah laughed (Genesis 18:12).

Jesus knew suffering too. He lost loved ones. John the Baptist was beheaded for a sinful woman's vanity. And Jesus went away alone to mourn. He was constantly let down by those closest to Him. His mother didn't quite understand. His kindred apparently misunderstood altogether. His disciples bickered, misinterpreted, and failed. One betrayed Him. And on the night when He most needed the comfort of others, the three closest to Him couldn't even stay awake. Three times He asked for deliverance. Three times He was answered no. He was accused of crimes He never committed, was condemned, and executed—not quickly, but slowly and painfully. Then when the agony was at its worst, He cried, "My God, My God, why hast Thou forsaken Me?" (Matthew 27:46).

However much we might wish it different, we are no more immune to suffering and death than our non-Christian friends. Christians die from twenty-story falls, just as non-

Christians. Christians get cancer, heart disease, and have birth defects, just as non-Christians. Christian parents lose children to leukemia and drunk drivers, just as non-Christian parents. Christians are raped. Christians starve. Christians lose their jobs. Christians are maimed and die on battlefields, in slums, in prisons, and in concentration camps. As Christians we hurt. We mourn. We struggle with long-term problems that appear to have no answers and no relief.

In such moments poking around the *whys* and the *whats* offers more false guilt than peace, more frustration than comfort. No one need compound his suffering by asking, "What have I done to deserve this?"

A better question remains.

WHAT AM I GOING TO DO ABOUT IT?

Someone has observed that peace comes not from the absence of conflict in life but from the ability to cope with it. Coping, handling, surviving—such things seem almost impossible after a torpedo strike.

What can you do when travail is too hard, the situation too hopeless and useless? How can you go on when it seems so pointless? How can you pray when God's presence and His promises seem null and void?

Coping may not be as hard as it looks, however. For the most part, it begins with a choice. We choose to make our suffering either good or bad.

In themselves, the things that happen to us are neutral. The disappointments in life, the illnesses, the accidents, the tragedies—all are incapable of killing faith. As much as they hurt, they don't have that great a power.

But our response to those events does.

It isn't what happens, but what we think about what happens that counts. Again, we choose. We choose to make our suffering a wellspring of bitterness. Or we choose to use it as a springboard to great sensitivity. We can start feeling sorry for ourselves, strike out to kill the pain, and walk away alone. Or we can turn to Jesus.

THE BITTERNESS OPTION

Systemic lupus. It's a painful, degenerative disease. And she had it. Why?

Sin? Pain washed over her joints and through her body

because she had committed some great and terrible sin. *Chastening?* She was in a wheelchair because God was chastening her for some reason. *Satanic attack?* Her kidneys were bleeding because of a Satanic attack. *Refining?* Seizures shook her body because God was refining her. *Testing her faith?* She couldn't hold a spoon or button buttons because God was testing her faith.

For ten years she endured. Then one day she told herself there was no faith left. Slowly, deliberately she swallowed a month's supply each of three strong medicines. And then she lay down to die.[1]

Bitterness. The word resounds with hostility and acidity. It is gall and wormwood eating away our inner selves until only a shell remains. If you've ever once given in to it, you know the feeling and the festering.

The Bible refers to it as a root (Hebrew 12:15).

It digs in, entwines itself around our tender parts, and sucks up all our strength, all our power. Any joys that come our way become grapes of poison. And each new frustration, no matter how small, comes saturated with the venom of cobras. We struggle half-heartedly against it, so that outwardly we at least look no worse than others. But inwardly we're an open grave.

Bitterness almost inevitably comes when we focus on *whys* and *whats.* Such questions are little more than attempts to pass the blame. When the tragic happens it's easier to blame someone—ourselves, our mates, God—than it is to deal realistically with the problem.

It's an old, old evasion—one long used by Satan. When somone suffers undeservedly, he immediately begins his whisper attack. *Why? What great and terrible sin have you committed?* None. *Then it must be God's fault. Where was He at Auschwitz? Where was He that your baby should be deformed . . . have progeria . . . die?* When a killer in Chicago beat eight nurses to death, a bitter relative asked, "Where was God when this happened? I'll tell you what I think. I

---

1. This story belongs to Merrily Anderson. For her telling of it, especially how she discovered God to be sovereign even over death, see her article "My Wilderness of Pain and Suffering," *Christianity Today* (22 January 1982):22-23.

think God is dead. He had a heart attack. He doesn't care about us."[2]

The argument looks and sounds good. So the adversary sharpens it into three prongs. The first prong says, "If God is God, He is not good. If God is good, He is not God." The second says, "God is love, but His love isn't one that bears any resemblance to what people normally call love." The third says, "Maybe God didn't do anything about it because He couldn't. Maybe He's imperfect. Maybe He just can't do everything."

Yet God is both God and good. His love is the true love that human love can only reflect. And He can do everything. When at last He spoke to Job, it was not to answer him but to thunder out:

> Where were you when I laid the foundation of the earth!
> Tell Me, if you have understanding,
> Who set its measurements, since you know?
> Or who stretched the line on it?
> On what were its bases sunk?
> Or who laid its cornerstone,
> When the morning stars sang together,
> And all the sons of God shouted for joy?
>
> Or who enclosed the sea with doors,
> When, bursting forth, it went out from the womb;
> When I made a cloud its garment,
> And thick darkness its swaddling band,
> And I placed boundaries on it,
> And I set a bolt and doors,
> And I said, "Thus far you shall come, but no farther;
> And here shall your proud waves stop"?
>
> (Job 38:4-11)

Faith is easy as long as we agree basically with what God is doing in our lives. But when things happen differently—when we feel cheated or robbed of something that we think ought to be ours—defiance creeps in. We cultivate rebellion in the dark corners of ourselves. Then bitterness flowers, full and ugly.

Once started, the life of bitterness offers its own rewards. In his fantasy narrative *The Singer*, Calvin Miller tells of a

---

2. Carl W. Berner, *Why Me, Lord? Meaning and Comfort in Times of Trouble* (Minneapolis: Augsburg, 1973), p. 48.

man for whom healing and happiness are contradictory. The man is a miller with one hand badly scarred and crippled. The Singer (Christ) offers to heal the miller. But the miller enjoys his mutilation too much for wholeness. He rolls on the floor, moaning, revelling in his deformity. When he opens his eyes to see why The Singer hasn't joined his pity party, The Singer is gone.[3]

Bitterness and spiritual survival. Any increase in one always results in a decrease to the other.

THE TRANSFORMING OPTION

Divorce. A word of endings, a word for helplessness. *Doubly so now,* Steve thought. He lay in bed crying, too ill to move and all alone. The pillow where once she rested her head was empty. He didn't know which hurt more, his sickness or the memory of her multiple adulteries. Even at that, she had insisted on the divorce, not he.

I love her, he thought. *Why doesn't she love me?* In his mind images jumbled. The emptiness in the pit of his stomach that came when the division was final. Rage when the life insurance company wouldn't let him change the beneficiary to his policy without her permission. Sadness that the house, their house, was up for sale. And impotence, for now he would have no children.

His Bible lay beside him. He picked it up and began to read. Then a verse caught his attention. "In everything give thanks; for this is God's will for you in Christ Jesus" (1 Thessalonians 5:18). It didn't make sense, but he'd try.

"Thank you, God, for all the bad things in my life. Thank you for this sickness. Thank you for my divorce. Thank you that I have to sell my home. Thank you I'll never have children."

He pulled the Bible closer and read on.

In the months that followed, Steve read the Bible through. He accepted the support of good friends—one especially who often dropped by late at night just to shoot pool and talk. He went on a diet and started getting back in shape. He went everywhere he was asked to go. And he decided to be in church for every service. He wouldn't lead in anything. But he could and would be the best pew sitter in church.

---

3. Calvin Miller, *The Singer* (Downers Grove, Ill.: InterVarsity, 1975), pp. 73-77.

Nine months passed, and his church started a single-again class for the widowed and divorced. Steve found himself telling the other class members, "If you ever need help, or someone to talk to, no matter when, call me."

One day a young widow with three preschool children called. Her car wouldn't start. Could he possibly get it going? It sounded like the one thing he could fix, so he said, "Sure." Something nice began that day. In time Steve found himself married again, with his own house, and with three growing daughters to daddy.

God did not design us to be "crushed Christians"—people who have given up on life and themselves as worthless. If we want, we can choose to become bitter. Or we can choose to be transformed, as Steve was.

In spite of what we've so long assumed, undeserved suffering is not the antithesis of life. We are prone to believe that suffering detracts from life. We think pain should be avoided at all costs. If it can't be eradicated, it ought to at least be medicated. So we wander from doctor to doctor, church to church, counselor to counselor, seeking some means—any means—to end the pain. And consequently we lose our chance to show what we're made of, to reveal our restraint, our dignity, our courage, our growth.

True, pain is not pleasant. It is neither enjoyable nor pretty. But it fertilizes our lives in a basic and necessary way. It gives us the nutrients we need for growth, strength, and spiritual reproduction. We learn who we are and what our relationship to God really is—not in the run-of-the-mill good days but in our wilderness of pain and suffering.

Several years ago an agricultural missionary told of an unusually severe drought in southern India. When the water was gone the first trees to wither and die were not those on the plains but those along the canals. Why? The trees by the canals normally had abundant water and had not developed the deep root system the water-scarce plains trees had developed.[4]

So it is in our lives. We gain strength and maturity more through suffering than through prosperity or temporary happiness. We sometimes want instant maturity or some six point checklist for spiritual perfection. But God doesn't work

---

4. Lowell R. Ditzen, *The Storm and the Rainbow* (New York: Holt, Rinehart & Winston, 1959), p. 15.

that way. As one observed, "What we call adversity, God calls opportunity; what we call tribulation, God calls growth."

It is only when the bottom is knocked out of our world that we discover the underlying foundations of God's world, which cannot be destroyed by anything that happens in time.

No one goes through life without suffering major disappointments. When they come it's normal to feel anger, hurt, and despair. It's OK to admit that you hurt. It's OK to admit that you can't cope with that hurt. It's OK to run to the Father.

How to Handle Undeserved Suffering

What are the practicalities?

First, accept what is. Accept it because it is. Stop clutching at what is not. Someone has said that acceptance is the first step to overcoming any misfortune. What does acceptance mean? It does *not* mean approval. We are not required to relish our hurts and count them good. Acceptance *does* mean that we liberate ourselves from worship of what once was but is no longer. Don't play "If only." Don't try to live in the past. Embrace reality. Come to grips with what is.

Second, be honest with God. Don't try to hide your feelings or your pain from Him. It's far better to tell God you think He blew it than to pretend everything is all right when you and He both know it isn't. You can hide your wounds from others but not from Him. So why put up a pretense? Let Him transform your worst feelings into something altogether new.

Third, ask Him to remove any root of bitterness. Disappointment that He didn't arrange things better, or anger that what we received was so far from what we wanted, are prime breeding grounds for mental revolt. As much as you can, steer clear. Confess any bitterness without trying to justify it. Don't cling to the past and to pain. Don't keep your spirit dwarfed at its moment for growth. Reach for wholeness instead.

Fourth, expect stumblings. Recovery from tragedy takes time. Expect that: Expect to occasionally fall, especially at first. And expect to keep on trying. The pain probably won't go away overnight. But it will go away—bit by bit, day by day. Winter doesn't last forever. Its grip is regularly ripped away by the coming of spring.

Fifth, make it a matter of give, not take. A pastor went to visit a little girl who was losing her sight. In fear she cried, "Pastor, God is taking my sight!" The pastor wisely responded, "Don't let Him take it—give it to Him." Make your suffering an altar. Make it an act of worship. Give it to God freely and completely.

Sixth, remember you're not alone. You are a part of a fellowship of sufferers, a common brotherhood in pain. Not all suffer alike. Not all suffer from the same causes. But all suffer. Indeed, when the pain is great and you need guidance, to whom do you go? Not to the one who has lived all his life carefree, but to the one who has weathered the dark night of the soul.

Finally, remember that God is still in control. Though suffering, pain, fear, and death assail us, He is still in the driver's seat. In his book *Why Me Lord? Meaning and Comfort in Times of Trouble* Carl W. Berner says, "Tribulations never come alone. God always comes with them. He has His hands in them. And those hands are strong and trustworthy. They will never let go. In every trouble He holds out His hands and whispers, 'Friend, take hold and hang on. Together we'll make it.'"[5] The suffering you face, even when it's the worst thing that can happen to you, does not come as God's backhand, but with His special presence. He loves us. He cares for us. And He does not change if we respond badly. We are still His chosen own.

LIFE IS A DRAMA

At least according to Malcolm Muggeridge it is.

In an interview he compared our suffering to that of the king in Shakespeare's play *King Lear*.

> In that drama there was this old king, suffering. I have imagined that two ladies go to the performance—two very humane ladies—and they really feel indignant that a poor old man should be made to suffer in that way. And then they meet Shakespeare in the eternal shades, and they say to him, "Why did you allow that poor old man to suffer like that?" He says, "Yes, I could have given the old man a sedative at the end of Act I, but it wouldn't have been a play."
>
> It sounds stupid, but actually I have found that in trying to get at this business of suffering, this analogy is enormously

---

5. Berner, p. 16.

helpful. Because if you did eliminate suffering from *King Lear*, there would be no play! And similarly with our life, we would learn nothing—we would know nothing at all. We would be utterly helpless and hopeless. *Understand that life is drama.*[6]

---

6. James and Elizabeth Newby, *Between Peril and Promise* (Nashville: Nelson, 1984), p. 11. Used by permission.

3
NO ONE BATS 1,000

Some time ago in a library I ran across a book entitled *Free to Be Human*. I liked the title, so I thumbed through the book. Unfortunately the contents didn't appear to live up to the title, so I reshelved the book and wandered on.

The title stuck with me though—free to be human. What did it mean? What would I want it to mean?

It seems to me that the most human thing I do is make mistakes. I am imperfect. I bungle, botch, fizzle, flub, and sometimes downright fail.

So free to be human means free to make mistakes, free to bat less than 1,000, free to lose.

Free or not, I do those things. We all do. As I understand it, perfection is in short supply among humankind. Psalm 53 says, "God has looked down from heaven upon the sons of men, to see if there is anyone who understands, who seeks after God. Every one of them has turned aside; together they have become corrupt; there is no one who does good, not even one" (Psalm 53:2-3).

What does it mean? Among other things, it means that true perfection is a trifle beyond our reach. (See what Paul had to say about this subject in Philippians 3:12.)

Failure and Spiritual Survival

We live, however, in what one has called a win/lose culture. We live in a society that persists in dividing people up into successes and duds. In a recent television commercial a frustrated little girl snarls, "I hate to lose!" Then her father calmly tells her how to win against tooth decay by using the advertised brand of toothpaste.

In itself the commercial is a humorous diversion on the way to the refrigerator. Yet in a larger sense it epitomizes the worship we accord achievement. Look at the heroes of our age—actors, musicians, superstars, sport figures, entrepreneurs—successes of all shapes, sizes, and flavors. We sing an unofficial national anthem of "Winning is everything, losing is less than nothing."

Small wonder we feel the pressure to win—somehow, some way. We forget that for every winner there also is a loser. He may be us. And that hurts. Because in our society, loser equals impotent, inadequate, second class, lesser-to-no status.

We forget that no one is uniformly successful. None of us is a whiz at everything. Rather each of us is a jumbled up mixture of success and failure. Look at baseball. We immortalize players like Mantle, Mays, Aaron, and Ruth; but how perfect were they? In an eighteen-year career Mickey Mantel batted a .289. Willy Mays in twenty-two years batted a .302. Home run king Hank Aaron batted a .305. Even the legendary Babe Ruth batted only a .342, and in the process struck out 1,330 times.[1] That's a countable hit only one out of every three times at bat. No one bats 1,000.

That is the problem. What do you do when your most cherished dreams lie smashed by your own error? What do you do when in all that's important to you, life brands you inept and incompetent? What do you do when your best laid plans vanish like an early morning mist? What do you do when your future looks blank, your present dismal, and your past a nightmare?

---

1. Statistics from *Baseball Encyclopedia*, ed. Joseph L. Reicher (New York: Macmillan, 1982).

LOSER'S LIMP

One response—one to be avoided—is to develop loser's limp.

It began as a sports term to describe what happens when a player starts limping to have an excuse for not doing better. A failure he doesn't want to face confronts him. So he limps as an evasion. Without the limp he is threatened with responsibility. With it he feels absolved.

Loser's limp is a refuge when the face of failure is so terrifying that we would do anything to avoid its frown. Loser's limp is giving up and quitting—sometimes even before the game begins. Loser's limp is avoiding failure by saying nothing, doing nothing, and being nothing.

I've never lost a race for public office. I've never lost a boxing match. I've never lost the lead role in a television series. And I've never lost a record contract. But then again, I've never run for public office, never been in a boxing match, never auditioned for an acting role, and never tried for a record contract.

Loser's limp. I never failed because I never tried.

But I can't let others know that. I can't let them suspect that I'm anything less than perfect and successful. So I hide my weaknesses and failures. I put up a false front; I deal in appearances. I maintain a facade of winning. I build a crust of subterfuge lest others discover my flaws and reject me. The thicker I make the crust, the more separate and lonely I feel.

I wonder how God can love me. I can hide from others. I can hide sometimes from myself. But surely He sees what a failure and hypocrite I really am. How can He care for me?

Or I blame God. After all, He made me. If I am a loser in a land of winners, it must be His fault. What have I ever done to Him to be treated so?

My loser's limp—run, hide, and make excuses.

FAILING SUCCESSFULLY

Failing succesfully is the opposite of loser's limp. What does it mean though? What does it mean to lose? What does it mean to succeed? Is winning really everything? How can you do both at the same time?

We usually define these by each other. A failure is someone unsuccessful. A success is someone who didn't fail. A failure is a loser—inferior. A success is a winner—superior. Those definitions create more problems than they solve, though. They totally ignore the fact that some fail successfully while others succeed failingly.

A successful failure is someone who through his failure grows. Contrary to popular belief life is not a cosmic scoreboard revealing our win/loss record. In fact, life does not require us to win at all. It asks us instead to grow, to become, to be what God calls us to be. We are not all called to be quarterbacks, Mr./Ms. Americas, wealthy, owners of large expensive houses, and members of the country club. We are all called to grow in Christlikeness.

A failed winner is someone who has success without satisfaction. It is Janis Joplin wondering, "Now that I'm here, where am I?" It is J. Robert Oppenheimer, the man who led the research team that designed the atom bomb, looking back at his achievements about a year before his death and saying, "They leave on the tongue only the taste of ashes."

We somehow forget that wholeness of life is a gift, not an achievement. Success seldom brings what we expect. We achieve fame and fortune only to find also loneliness, isolation, and heartbreak. Or we find in failure the promise of a new beginning.

The Bad Friday Perspective

It was a miserable day—a day of endings.

The day before had been a national holiday but not a normal eat, drink, and be merry one. The Master kept saying all those weird things. By mealtime He'd made everyone uneasy—especially Peter.

Then He had wanted to walk in the garden. That seemed unreasonable to Peter. A good night's rest would have been more sensible.

In the garden Peter had dozed, only to awake with a start when the police came. It was all the sleep Peter had that night.

The police took the Master then. And in spite of all Peter had earlier claimed, he hadn't stopped them. He could only tag along in the dark. Three times in the night someone asked if Peter knew the Master. Three times he denied it.

Now today—unheard-of weather, unnatural darkness, and the same folks who only days ago shouted joyous greetings now howled for the Master's death. There He was, being executed for a crime He didn't commit, and nobody could stop it.

Tears ran down Peter's face. The Master was dead. It was all over. There wasn't any more hope, any more plans, any more purpose, any more anything. The failure was complete and final.

Peter shook his head. It was time to let go, return home, and see if any strands of the old life could be picked up. If home would have him.

We've all had Black Fridays—days when all our dreams, all our hopes, were crucified on the brutal trees of our own failures. All that Black Friday left was an overpowering impression that failure was forever; that no matter how hard we tried, God's first plan for our lives was totally destroyed. Black Friday symbolizes the illusion of a permanent end.

Black Friday is the slum tenement of life, overrun with the rats of self-destruction, self-wounding, and self-hate. With one hand we beat ourselves for the failure that brought us there. With the other we cling to the event, refusing to move on to anything new until the old is sufficiently punished. Since that never happens, we stay. Soon Black Friday becomes our home, the place we know. We draw comfort from it, cherish it, and fear leaving it. Who knows what Sunday might bring?

The Easter Perspective

If Friday was the worst day in Peter's life, Sunday didn't begin much better. The shock was beginning to wear off. Plans were taking shape—third-rate plans, no-hope plans, go-home plans. That didn't matter. They at least gave him something to do. That didn't matter either. Doing was better than quitting. But what real good is doing in a world where Black Fridays come?

Then Mary came. Wasn't it bad enough they had killed the Master? Now they've stolen His body as well! Peter ran to the grave and saw it for himself. What more could they do? Peter's shoulders drooped as he returned to where they were staying.

Mary came again later in the day. But by then Peter had wrapped himself so thickly in despair that her words were just sounds without meanings.

Alive? He's alive. Who? And so what?

Jesus? Mary, you're not making sense. He's dead. I saw it.

His body's gone, but they stole it. It's all over. Don't you understand?

Good grief! You two also. I thought you had gone to Emmaus. I don't believe it. I know you loved Him and miss Him. I do too. But He's dead. Don't you understand? He's dead!

Then He came. Black Friday became Good Friday. And Easter swallowed the world.

Seen from the Easter perspective, no failure is forever. And no failure is final. Someone said, "If you have made mistakes, even serious ones, there's always another chance. Real failure is not falling down but staying down."

In *Another Chance: How God Overrides Our Big Mistakes*, Dr. Haddon Robinson tells of a 1919 Rose Bowl game between Georgia Tech and the University of California. Shortly before halftime a California player, Roy Riegels, recovered a fumble and in the confusion started running the wrong way. Sixty-five yards later, just before he would have scored for the opposite team, one of his own teammates tackled him.

In the halftime period, Roy sat in a corner and cried. Everyone waited for Coach Nibs Price to speak. Finally, three minutes before playing time, the coach said, "The same men that played the first half will start the second."

All the players except Roy went out onto the field.

Coach Price went over to where Roy slumped and said again, "The same men that played the first half will start the second."

Roy looked up and said, "Coach, I can't. I've ruined you. I've ruined the University of California. I've ruined myself. I can't face that crowd in the stadium."

Coach Price reached out and put his hand on Roy's shoulder and said, "Son, get up and go on back; the game is only half over."[2] Few men have ever played with the fierceness and dedication that Roy Riegels played that second half.

No failure is final until we will it to be. No matter how black it looks, it's only halftime—a time for beginning new and fresh things.

The Values of Failure

Does it seem warped to speak of failure having value?

---

2. Reprinted by permission from Denver Seminary's quarterly magazine *Focal Point*, vol. 3, no. 4, October-December 1983.

Sometimes that seems the same as telling a drowning man the water is good for him. Yet failure does have value.

Failure has value as a teacher—possibly the best one we'll ever have. Think of the things you do from walking and reading to playing the piano and repairing your car. Each skill was learned by trying, failing, and trying again. Where would you be if you had refused to walk until you were certain you would not fail? We gain our most treasured abilities through long practice and frequent failure.

Failure has value because it reminds us we are human. Failure shows us that in spite of our successes, we are not gods. We are not omni-successful universe conquerors but frail gardeners with definite limitations.

Failure has value because it gives us a fresh opportunity to reexamine our dreams and aspirations. Perhaps the success we hoped for was too unrealistic or too self-serving. Perhaps the battle was a false one, unnecessary from the start. Or perhaps the only way we could have succeeded would have been at the price of a broken relationship. Failure gives us time for reflection and reevaluation.

Failure has value because it opens the door for a revived relationship with God. Failure on our own turf always leaves open the chance of success on God's. When we are weak, He is strong. When we count it all as loss, he can guide us on. Falling on our faces hurts, but He can make the loss a stepping-stone to maturity.

Finally, failure has value in making us whole. It brings freedom. Having failed—not once, but many times—we are free to fear losing no longer. We are free to take risks and free to be ourselves. We can shed the burden of perfection—and the hypocrisy, false fronts, and self-imposed prison it represents. We need no longer play spiritual charades. Rather we are free to accept and be accepted—warts and all.

How to Fail Successfully

How does one learn to fail successfully?

First, be kind to yourself. In spite of what you may think, you have value. You have enough value that Christ died for you. You can reject the thought, run from it, hide from it. Your reaction changes nothing; in God's eyes you have value. So don't let failure tie you in knots. Relax. Loosen your reins. You have the right to fail. Give yourself permission to be imperfect, permission to bat less than 1,000, permission to be human.

Second, abandon the use of false yardsticks. All too often we judge ourselves and others by superficial standards—abilities, bankbooks, friends, results. One side of the mark we declare to be winners; the other side contains the losers. The problem is that God doesn't gauge our success by our talents and/or how we use them, by the greatness or smallness of our financial statement, by the number or kind of friends we have, or by the results (or lack thereof) we achieve in any given field. Contrast those false standards against growth in Christlikeness and seeking His kingdom first. Go easy on yourself. Stop raking yourself over the coals for failures in areas that don't matter anyway.

Third, acknowledge your imperfections. Face failure honestly; don't fake success. This is important for three reasons. One, "perfect" people are frozen in mediocrity; imperfect people are free to grow. Two, acknowledging imperfections frees us from spending enormous emotional amounts on a defense budget designed to keep people away. And three, the more we admit to being the cause of our own problems the more we can empathize with others who are the same.

Fourth, don't give up the ship. Never use failure as an excuse to quit. You may not be able to reverse the consequence of your failure. The loss may well remain lost, the damage damaged. But you can make a fresh start. After all, God specializes in new beginnings.

Fifth, learn from your failures. Erwin Lutzer has written an excellent book entitled *Failure: The Back Door to Success.*[3] I like that title. Failure can be the back door to success; but only if we learn from it. Exploit your failures. Mine them for insight and understanding. Don't waste them.

Sixth, take your time. We live in an age of instant coffee, instant food, instant television, and—with winning game show contestants—instant wealth. Consequently we look for instant growth, instant overcoming. Like most of the really important things in life, learning to use failure successfully is a long-term process. Despite what you may have heard, you won't be demerited for taking a while to get there. You have all your life to grow. So give yourself some breathing space.

Finally, commit it all to God, and leave it there. Don't resurrect the failures and mistakes of yesterday to make you miserable today.

3. Erwin Lutzer, *Failure: The Back Door to Success* (Chicago: Moody, 1975).

4
GUILT—FRIEND OR FOE

Black.
A hole in myself.

It's swimming through the water to eat me. Faster and faster.

I try to escape.

It grabs my feet and pulls me under.

Through the water I hear it rumbling, "Pay, pay, now you will pay." And it laughs as my lungs burn for air.

Guilt. Is it friend or foe? Angel or demon?

At first I think it must be foe. It threatens me, and I fear it. It whispers that the soul that sins must die and that the wild seeds I plant will surely bear a harvest. The glee in its voice makes me feel lonely, isolated, and empty. I must be drowning spiritually. I am far from shore, in deep water. The lifeguard looks the other way, alienated by my wilful, hateful ways. I turn on myself and shout, "Drown, baby, drown!"

Or is guilt a friend? Willard Gaylin, a psychoanalyst, calls guilt a "guardian of our goodness."[1] He's right. If it were not

---

1. Willard Gaylin, "On Feeling Guilty," *Atlantic Monthly* (January, 1979): 82.

for guilt I wouldn't be writing this now. I would be reading a novel, watching TV, or sleeping. If it weren't for guilt I would care nothing for you or for anyone except myself. I would freely satisfy my every whim. If it pleased me I would do evil, smile, and call it good. Or do good, frown, and call it evil. Without guilt, how would I know the difference? Or knowing it, would I care?

Which is it—friend or foe? At first it seems one. Then it seems the other. And I feel lost in confusion. What is guilt anyway? Why do I have it? Is it good, bad, or indifferent? Is it a psychological remnant of my upbringing that ought to be exorcised? Or is it a valid experience to be faced with courage and honesty?

WHAT IS GUILT?

The word comes from the Anglo-Saxon word *gylt*. It means "to pay." Certainly that seems appropriate. Whenever I hear the voice of guilt, it shouts of a fine levied and payment expected.

But the question remains. What is guilt?

On one level there is legal guilt, which might be defined as an act of legal or moral wrongdoing. Joe makes a habit of speeding. Mary takes small items that don't belong to her. John owns his own business and conveniently forgets to record payments received in cash. Each is guilty of legal sin. But that doesn't mean they feel guilty.

A deeper level is remorseful guilt. It comes when an act of legal guilt is brought into internal focus. It is when Joe, Mary, or John says to himself, "I have done wrong." It isn't just a matter of fear, like the manipulation achieved with the childhood threat, "I'm going to tell Daddy/Mommy on you." Nor is it a matter of shame, where we dwell on what others will think of us when they find out. Rather the emphasis is on an inner awareness of wrongdoing.

According to Gaylin, guilt also is "a form of self-disappointment."[2] What he means is that we carry within us a set of standards of what we ought to be and do. When we violate that internal law, we betray ourselves. We betray God. And we hurt.

---

2. Ibid., p. 81.

How Guilt Works

As a boy I was a Cub Scout and loved it. I also loved candy bars and comic books, neither of which was overly abundant in my home. One day a friend and I decided to get some of these on our own. But our options were limited. We had no money. None was available from parents. Because of an earlier experience I had vowed never to steal again. The situation looked impossible.

We found our answer in pop bottles. Pop bottles could be returned for the deposit. Then we would have money for candy and comics. But we had no pop bottles.

We thought about that awhile and came up with a plan to get them. We put on our scout caps, took my friend's wagon, and walked a few blocks over from his house. Then we began knocking on doors. We told who ever answered that we were collecting pop bottles for a Scout drive.

After fifteen minutes and a wagon full of bottles, we reached a house where the man at home eyed us suspiciously. He wanted to know our names, the name of our troop, and the purpose of the drive. Before he would give us anything, he wanted to call and check us out. We lied hastily, and no doubt obviously. He went in to call a bogus number, and we took off running.

Fear set in. What would happen if my parents found out? My imagination supplied graphic visions of the spanking to end all spankings. Thoughts of shame came. What if someone told my den mother? Would I be drummed out of the Cub Scouts?

In the week that followed, guilt was like a splinter in my soul that had festered. I knew I had done wrong—not because I would get a spanking or be ashamed—but because the act itself was wrong. I had lied. More, I had lied to achieve a gain. In effect, I had broken my vow not to steal again. I was guilty. I had made myself untrustworthy. I had acted not out of weakness or ignorance but with intentional deliberation. It had not been oversight but active decision. It was time for a trial.

THE COURTROOM OF THE I

The guard compelled me into the courtroom and took me to my lawyer.[3] We stood as the judge entered. The judge

---

3. I am heavily indebted to William Justice for the inspiration and form of this section. See his book *Guilt and Forgiveness* (Grand Rapids: Baker, 1980), chapter 5, "We Go on Trial," pp. 67-80. Used by permission.

wore my face. So did the prosecutor, the guards, the arresting officer, and the jury. I could expect no mercy there. I knew then all was lost.

The prosecutor stood to begin his case. He looked mean, mad, and hard. For a moment he glared at me. Then he read the charge, "Your Honor, the courtroom of the I charges Larry Neagle with four counts of deliberate transgression.

"The charges are (1) lying, (2) gaining money by that lie, (3) vow breaking, and (4) premeditated theft."

Behind me someone gasped. Another voice called, "He's guilty! Make him pay!"

The judge smirked and said, "All in good time, friend. All in good time."

The trial began.

The prosecution called its first witness—my friend. He came weeping into the courtroom. He stopped when he saw me and cried out, "It's all his fault, Your Honor. We were playing happily when he said he knew how to get money for comics and candy. It was his scheme, Your Honor."

Behind me someone yelled, "Guilty!" And another, "Hanging is too good for him!"

The next witness was a little old lady who had given us a carton of bottles. "Yes, Your Honor. He's the boy. He told me he was collecting pop bottles for a drive. I thought he was probably lying, but . . . What are young people coming to these days?"

The next witness said, "He's the one, Your Honor. Actually I didn't give him any bottles. I didn't have any. But the Scouts are a good cause. I gave him some loose change instead."

One after another the people I'd lied to accused me, until at last the man who wanted to check us out took the stand. "That's the one, Your Honor. Said he was collecting bottles for a Scout drive. I knew he was a thief when I laid eyes on him. Nervous mouth. And he wouldn't look me in the eye. When I questioned him, his answers contradicted themselves. And when I went in to call his troop, he ran away."

The prosecutor smiled. "That's our case, Your Honor."

The judge turned to dismiss the jury for a verdict.

"What about my defense?" I squeaked.

The judge scowled and glanced at his watch. "Waste of taxpayers' time, if you ask me. Make it brief."

My defense counsel stood. He too wore my face. He looked shifty and untrustworthy.

"My client is innocent of the charges, Your Honor."

Someone laughed and said, "We've heard that one before."

The judge looked bored. He twiddled his thumbs and said, "On what basis?"

"On the basis of mistaken identity, your Honor. All the witnesses are mistaken. It wasn't my client who lied about the pop bottles. It was another little boy who looked like him."

Several of the jurors guffawed.

My lawyer ignored them. For a few minutes he spoke about my hypothetical twin. I almost believed him.

"Come, come, counselor," the judge interrupted. "You're going to have to do better than that. If this continues we'll have to charge the boy with a count of perjury as well."

My lawyer looked worried. He shuffled some papers on the table in front of him. Finally, he cleared his throat and said, "Your Honor, my client is still innocent. After all, it really wasn't his fault. If his friend hadn't urged him on . . ."

"I object," shouted the prosecutor. "His friend isn't on trial here."

"Objection sustained," the judge grunted.

"But it wasn't my client's fault," my lawyer whined. "It was all his friend's idea."

"I said, 'Objection sustained,' counselor!"

Beads of perspiration formed on my lawyer's lip. "If my client's parents had given him the money he asked for . . ."

"Objection. His parents are not on trial here either. The defendant can't continue to blame others. He did it himself. No one forced him."

"Sustained."

My lawyer turned to the jury. "Look at my client."

I tried to hide.

"He's a fine looking boy," my lawyer continued. "In the week since the alleged theft, he's been a model son. He's even said 'sir' and 'ma'am' to his parents. Surely such conduct deserves consideration."

"Objection, Your Honor. His conduct since the crime does not absolve him from the crime."

"Sustained."

"But Your Honor, everyone knows that boys will be boys."

"Objection."

"Sustained."

"But Your Honor," my lawyer pleaded, "surely you aren't going to convict my client. He's a boy with a love for candy and comics. He can't help that. Don't punish him for urges he was born with!"

"Obj—"

"Never mind," the judge interrupted. "It's obvious there's no real defense to present. Such lies and evasions. I would be shocked if I hadn't heard it all before."

He paused and turned to the bailiff. "Take the jury next door for their deliberations."

"There's no need, Your Honor," the foreman of the jury said. "We're all agreed. The boy is guilty."

For a moment all was silent. Then everyone in the courtroom began shouting, "Guilty! Guilty! Guilty!" The room reeled, and I fell to the floor. Everyone's finger was pointing at me. And their chant changed. "Make him pay. Make him pay. Make him pay!"

The judge stared at me without mercy. "Larry Neagle, you are found guilty as charged. You are henceforth deemed untrustworthy to others and to God. You have shown yourself to be an habitual offender. Therefore I sentence you to a life of feeling ill at ease and worthless. Regardless of what others think of you, you will always know yourself to be a hypocrite—empty, beneath notice, and good for nothing. This court orders you to confess this transgression to your parents and abide by their decision."

I tried not to cry. What could I say? I knew I was guilty.

My lawyer leaned over. Why wouldn't he look me in the eye?

"Cheer up," he said. "I think we can bargain for a lighter sentence."

Guilt and Spiritual Survival

How then does guilt affect spiritual survival?

Up to this point guilt and its effect on us has been healing, life preserving, even wholesome. It has functioned like a smoke detector, alerting us to imminent danger and the need for direct action.

Contrary to what one pop psychologist claims, guilt is not a "useless" or "futile" emotion.[4] But our responses to it frequently are. Guilt demands a decision from us. Shall we face the guilt and its cause and move on into wholeness? Or will we evade the issues and place our spiritual lives in danger?

---

4. Wayne W. Dyer, *Your Erroneous Zones* (New York: Avon, 1977), p. 97.

The problem is that most of us would rather not face the sentence guilt assesses as it's given. So we try to plea bargain. We offer to swap for a more acceptable punishment. Or we try to jump bail, forgetting that wherever we go the court also goes.

Most of us are a little like the fellow in a parable told by Dr. John W. Drakeford.[5] A Jewish couple in Nazi Germany knew the time for their arrest was soon. They made an agreement with a one-legged veteran. In return for caring for their paralyzed son, the veteran would receive the lease on their apartment. Upon the couple's arrest, the veteran had the boy smuggled away to a mountain cabin. There the boy was abandoned to die. The veteran assured himself that he had fulfilled his part of the bargain and promptly sold the lease.

He awoke one morning shortly after to find a bump about the size of a pigeon's egg on his forehead. He pressed the bump in. Pop—it came out at the back of his skull. He gave it another push, and it appeared over his right ear. He pushed it again, and it came out on top of his head. He looked at it for a minute and decided to leave it alone. At least there it could be covered by his hat.

Like the man, we play games with our guilt trying to force it into a more acceptable sentence. And like the bump, our guilt refuses to be dismissed.

How do we try to bypass our guilt sentence? One way is by excuses. I tried several of those in my trial above. Most of these begin with, "Well, it's not really my fault because . . ." All of them stem from a basic unwillingness to recognize one's personal responsibility for destructive attitudes and actions.

Often the excuse evolves into blaming another. My friend blamed me, and I blamed him. We've followed that pattern since Adam blamed Eve. But passing the buck never works. Guilt pushed in here pops out there.

Sometimes we try to evade our guilt by projecting it onto others. A middle-aged man was convinced of his wife's unfaithfulness. He saw signs of it in her clothes, her posture, her use of the car, and in a thousand other little things. Confronted with her husband's suspicions, the wife was shocked, hurt, and able to prove her innocence. But the husband

---

5. John W. Drakeford, *Integrity Therapy* (Nashville: Broadman, 1967), p. 34. All rights reserved. Used by permission.

remained unconvinced. It became obvious later that he was the one who had been unfaithful. He popped his guilt bump in only to have it pop out in the belief that his wife was being unfaithful to him.

Sometimes we try to dodge guilt with defensive aggression. It hurts less to feel anger than guilt. So when something goes wrong we unleash our fury at those around us rather than face the reality of our own culpability. The "hot potato syndrome" sets in.[6] A man trying to fix his car's carburetor breaks off a piece of it into the machinery. Unable to cope with that failure he becomes enraged and beats a dent into the fender. A wife finds herself constantly annoyed and provoked by the little things in her husband's behavior. Could it be she cannot, or will not, face the answer to the question, What have I done wrong toward him? A man, sent by his wife to buy a carton of milk, runs over a loose nail and has a flat. He comes home with the milk and a snarled accusation—"It's all your fault!"

Another way of bypassing guilt involves paying a substitute debt. Consider a young high school student who in a moment of weakness engages in sexual misconduct. Shocked by her action and unable to endure it, she pushes the guilt bump in. But it has to pop out somewhere else. The feelings remain. In the courtroom of the I she knows she is guilty. She knows she must pay. So she confesses to an admired teacher that she has cheated on a test. She apologizes and offers to make amends. She does extra work, even personal favors. She tries to pay a substitute debt. But the guilt remains, because she has not dealt with the real transgression.

A variant of this occurs in those who appear to be excessively guilty. The pattern seems to be too much guilt over too small an infraction. Consider a middle-aged widow who continually seeks counseling from her pastor over trivial misdeeds. In the beginning he admires her sensitivity. Later he dreads seeing her at all. Is she an overscrupulous person whose standards are set too high? Or is there an unfaced guilt bump in her life? Such apparent dedication may be little more than an elaborate smoke screen for a major misdeed.

What happens when we try these evasions?

We find ourselves caught on a perpetual treadmill. We do something wrong. Guilt calls us up short, defining the wrong we've done. We ignore it, evade it, try to bury it. Fresh guilt

---

6. Gaylin, p. 82.

arises over that wrong. We ignore that. Fresher guilt arises. Soon we feel like prime candidates for the spiritual garbage heap.

The more we try to ease the penalty, the more it compounds daily. We begin a pattern of self-vindication and self-punishment. The problem is that the amount of self-punishment inflicted is rarely enough. Because of our steadfast refusal to face the issues, the inner court keeps crying, "More! More!" No wonder such an approach has been called "suicide on the installment plan"[7] and "the cycle of the damned."[8]

How to Make Constructive Use of Guilt

Arthur Becker in his book *Guilt: Curse or Blessing* says, "The voice of guilt seems always to speak two words: the dread word of punishment, and the sigh of longing for forgiveness."[9] Somehow, in spite of all we've done, a soft voice within us whispers, "Maybe . . ." And hope, more fragile than the flicker of a candle flame, quietly breathes the possibility of a return.

How can we return? How can we make constructive use of guilt?

First, recognize that guilt is a legitimate emotion. Pop psychology notwithstanding, guilt is not a useless emotion. Rather it is an early warning signal to save us from sin and self-defeat.

Second, examine guilt's roots. Don't play push the bump. Instead take a long look at the attitudes and actions causing the guilt. Be specific. Don't try to sidestep responsibility. This is a case of I-did-it, not it-happened-to-me. Unmask yourself. Face the cause honestly. This confronting who we are and what we've done is a necessary part of God's process of healing. Becoming whole again is painful. But it's far less painful than further fragmentation.

Third, accept forgiveness. God is offering it. The price? Confession, repentance, and possibly restitution. Confession—it's time to admit verbally to God the wrong we've committed. Repentance—we determine to turn away from the wrong

---

7. Justice, p. 88.
8. Ibid., p. 104.
9. Arthur Becker, *Guilt: Curse or Blessing* (Minneapolis: Augsburg, 1977), p. 67.

and to the right. And restitution—doing all we can to repair the damage we've created. Remember the promise of 1 John 1:9—"If we confess our sins, He is faithful and righteous to forgive us our sins and to cleanse us from all unrighteousness." Does it only work when we *feel* forgiven? No, the feelings don't matter. The fact is, we *are* forgiven.

Finally, forgive yourself. That's not as hard as it might seem. Nothing we've done, or can do, can put us beyond God's care, abilities, or love. Focus on these words: "Because God has forgiven me, I forgive me too." Then do it. After all, who are we to be holier than God?

5

WHAT DO I DO WITH THE MEMORIES?

It wasn't a pretty memory. Adultery never is. But there it was again, flashing across his mind, a sick souvenir of his life's most obscene moment. It occurred years ago. It was confessed. Reconfessed. Yet there it was again. Haunting him. Hurting him.

Why couldn't he forget?

He could forget names, birthdays, and important tasks. Why couldn't he forget this? It lurked continually on the edge of his awareness, waiting for any opportunity to break in and wreck his calm.

HAUNTING MEMORIES AND SPIRITUAL SURVIVAL

Painful memories. We all have them. Recollections of things—not imagined, not fantasy, not illusion—but all too real. What we did. What others did. Angers. Hurts. Injustices. Heartaches. Offenses. Shame. Troubles. Sometimes big, sometimes insignificant. Yet persistent. Painful. Memories so laden, so holding, so powerful that they can neither be forgotten nor escaped.

They come like a needle stuck on a record: repeating, repeating, repeating. Or like a broken VCR endlessly replaying that one definitive defeat, despair, dishonesty, or disaster. So that soon all our faith and confidence erodes into a heap of rubble.

Arthur Rouner says, "One of the hardest things we have to live with is our memories. One of our heaviest burdens is the past."[1] It also presents a major barricade for spiritual survival.

Just when we think things are going well—our equilibrium is back, our balance, our self-control—out pops that secret memory, tormenting and terrifying us. Pain fills us anew. And we flounder, like a swimmer with muscle cramps or a beached whale too tired to fight its way back to the sea.

If only the past could be erased, like a blackboard or a video cassette tape. Instead it flashes over and over on the screen of our minds. We try to change channels, but no matter what station we put it on, the program is the same, and we're the star. Small wonder David said, "For I know my transgressions, and my sin is ever before me" (Psalm 51:3).

The Problem of Forgetting

What makes us remember? What makes us forget?

The question isn't as academic as it sounds. If we can learn to forget, maybe we can learn how to rid ourselves of those unwanted memories once and for all. How do people forget? Is there any way painful memories can be ejected from our consciousness? Is there any way to break that continuous playing loop of video tape?

Some assume that not only is there a way to forget but also that we do it all the time. They speak of repression and suppression.

Repression, according to Ian M. L. Hunter, "refers to unconscious blocking of the recall of those experiences or activities which have potentiality for causing the person pain."[2] Sigmund Freud originated the concept and defined it in part as a "psychic flight from displeasure." "The essence of repression," he said, "lies simply in the function of rejecting and keeping something out of consciousness." The idea as used

---

1. Arthur R. Rouner, Jr. *Healing Your Hurts* (Nashville: Abingdon, 1978), p. 41.
2. Ian M. L. Hunter, *Memory: Facts and Fallacies* (Baltimore: Penguin, 1964), p. 232.

today refers to an unconscious process.

Suppression, on the other hand, is a conscious activity. According to John W. Drakeford, "Suppression refers to the deliberate mental activity by which the dirty linen basket of the mind is stuffed with the wrinkled and soiled rags of unworthy experience. The activity is consciously undertaken in much the same manner as the fussy housewife sorts the dirty laundry from the clean. This practice of evaluation against an ideal and conscious disposal is the distinctive suppression."[3]

Either way the idea is that we forget what we want to forget. The message is that if a memory is sufficiently painful (displeasurable) we will either unconsciously or consciously forget it.

This looks attractive, but neither repression nor suppression is an answer. Painful memories shoved into psychic stew boil back in some other form of poison. Neither repression nor suppression is universally effective.

What about those memories we can't get rid of? What about those emotionally super-charged memories that refuse to go? Evidently our unconscious isn't dealing too effectively with them. Nor can we deliberately shush them up. What are we to do about them?

WHAT MAKES US REMEMBER?

What we remember is influenced by three things. The first of these lies in the activities surrounding the original event. What were the circumstances of the event? Was it an act of sin that has left behind an undealt-with scar of guilt? Was it an embarrassing failure, an act of shame, a bitterly resented loss or suffering? Whatever it was, it happened to you in a context to generate overpowering emotion. The emotion comes not just from the event itself but also from all the supporting activities around it. Think of it in terms of a play. The event is the main character. But the main character is supported by a number of other characters, some major and some minor, so that the end results from the combined effort of all. All of the bit players around that memory combine to give it its emotional power—from the weather to a compilation of every other painful thing that happened in the vicinity

---

3. John W. Drakeford, *Integrity Therapy* (Nashville: Broadman, 1967), p. 55. All rights reserved. Used by permission.

of that event. The event, its surrounding activities, and how we perceive both of those all go into the remembering.

Second, remembering is influenced by our activities at the time of remembering. All it takes for a painful memory to steal center stage is for something—anything—in our present situation to tie to a similar thing in the event's situation. Anything can do it—a name, a word, a phrase, a song, a place, a person, an activity, a thought.

In time the tie of similar circumstance doesn't have to be conscious. It performs a vanishing trick. This is what happens when a child is learning to write. At first he is given letters to trace over or models to follow. Then the letters are made increasingly more fragmentary, the models given less and less often, until finally the child is able to draw the letters on a blank sheet. Likewise in the beginning a painful memory may be prompted by a consciously noted similarity of circumstances. After awhile even the vaguest of ties will set up a current of remembering, until at last the memory comes without cue and against our will.

The final factor in remembering is what we've done with the memory since the event occurred. Often with painful memories we are selective in what we remember. It is as if we were film directors viewing an important piece of movie footage. We experiment with different camera locations. We magnify and maximize, then reduce and minimize. In short, we embellish our painful memories. We don't make major changes, just colorings to make the event appear in its worst possible light.

With each remembrance we shade it a little darker. We add negative interpretations of the event: it happened because I'm a terrible person; God must be very angry with me; the future is completely shot. So that layer by layer vague misgivings and self-doubts are laquered to the event, proving to us our own worthlessness.

The Other Option

Forgetting isn't the answer. Common experience tells us that. We remember what we want to forget and forget what we want to remember. Unless we make a special effort, necessary names, important dates, and needed information vanish into oblivion. But painful memories we remember with technicolor vividness.

If forgetting isn't the answer, what is?

Why not be healed?

A painful memory is like a psychic wound. The original event lacerates our minds—puncturing, rending, slashing down to the very roots of self. It isn't fatal usually. No amputations are needed, at least when we let it heal normally and without infection. Problems come when we make a habit of picking at the scab, when we keep the wound ever fresh and infected.

Why do we do that?

Is it because that wounding event is somehow so important that we feel we need some memorial other than a nicely healed scar? Is it something so shameful that the only way we can make ourselves do sufficient penance is by continual remembering and shame? Or is it a loss so great that the only way we can keep the sense of it current is by keeping the wound renewed?

Whatever the reason, picking the scab—giving it continued psychic activity—only gives the wound added power to disrupt our lives. Why not disinfect it instead? If the memory itself can't be removed, why not at least take away the pain?

No one can look back without seeing something to regret—memories of deep hurt, deep fear, deep hate. We needn't try to run from those memories as if we could ever be some place where they aren't. Neither need we make an emotional scrapbook of them—collecting them, nurturing them, surrendering to them, becoming their prisoner.

We need to face them. We need to confront and haul them out into the light. Those painful memories are much like bumps in the night. They magnify themselves. But facing the memories, like flipping on a light, begins the act of healing.

LET THE PAST BE THE PAST

Past—as the old saying goes, that's what the word means: something that's over; something we need not return to. Yet all too often, return to it we do. We need to learn the art of letting the past be past.

Contrary to popular belief, people are not stuck with their pasts. At least not in the sense that would label them marred forever because of the bad things and the good things that have happened to them in life. Traumas—all the events that cause painful memories—almost never in themselves constitute sufficient cause of adult problems. They do represent a potential for problems—a potential that can be overridden.

We need not continue living yesterday today. We need not lose the joy that could be today in the festering of yesterday.

Who benefits from such actions?

In his book *Spiritual Depression* D. Martyn Lloyd-Jones says, "If you look at the past and are depressed, you're listening to the devil."[4] Satan is the one that likes for us to hang on to the rubbish of yesterday. He enjoys exhuming it, parading it before us at the worst possible moments. He doesn't want us to let the past be past, not when he can use it to keep us ever defeated, ever rebellious. As long as the enemy can keep us dwelling on the past he has won a victory in today.

Such dwelling on the past is unnatural and self-defeating.

How so?

Allowing ourselves to be miserable in the present because of some pain in the past is a sheer waste of time and energy. Think about it. The past cannot be recalled. Neither can we *do* anything about it. We can sit and be miserable, or we can go around in circles of regret. But neither changes anything. What has happened still has happened. Why do we waste time worrying about something we cannot change? We ought to dismiss such dwelling as irrational, a Satanic effort to defeat us.

Dwelling on the past also nullifies the power of time to heal. The psyche, like the body, can heal itself, if we leave the scab alone. But as long as we aggravate the sore—giving that long ago event today's power—we keep it infected.

Finally, dwelling on the past causes failure in the present. As long as our focus is on that past event, today gets little to no attention. As long as we are polarized to something that happened long ago, we won't be overly open to the potentialities present in today. Again according to D. Martyn Lloyd-Jones, "It is always wrong to mortgage the present by the past; it is always wrong to allow the past to act as a brake on the present. Let the dead past bury its dead."[5]

The apostle Paul knew how to let his dead past bury its dead. Look at his preconversion activities: holding coats while Stephen is stoned; raiding homes from Jerusalem to Damascus; and casting men, women, and children into prison merely

---

4. D. Martyn Lloyd-Jones, *Spiritual Depression* (Grand Rapids: Eerdmans, 1965), p. 75.
5. Ibid., p. 83.

for believing in Jesus. Yet of his past he said, "Brethren, I do not regard myself as having laid hold of it yet; but one thing I do: forgetting what lies behind and reaching forward to what lies ahead, I press on toward the goal for the prize of the upward call of God in Christ Jesus" (Philippians 3:13-14).

Whatever else Paul meant by that, it seems to suggest that it isn't the past that makes a person who he is; it's the present that gives him the opportunity to be who he will be. The event that caused that painful memory isn't all that important. It is like a match that starts a bonfire. Once the blaze is going, extinguishing the match won't help. The problem then isn't the match, but the fire. So the problem with painful memories isn't the event, but how we choose to feel and think about it. The way we choose to treat such memories is far more important than the events themselves.

The options are simple. We can give painful memories present reality and keep past suffering alive today. Or we can recognize that past events have only a past reality, a reality recoverable only in memory. They can never exceed that. The past, recalled, is only an invitee to our minds. It exists by our grace. And it never has more than a purely mental reality. The power of the past is only an illusion—an illusion that vanishes the moment you decide the past is past and not the present nor the future.

MAKE TODAY YOUR ALLY

Whatever the past was, the present is what matters. Put your effort into it.

How?

Do what you can in the present to make up for the past. Paul knew the value of this. Again referring to his past he said, "For I am the least of the apostles, who am not fit to be called an apostle, because I persecuted the church of God. But by the grace of God I am what I am, and His grace toward me did not prove vain; but I labored even more than all of them, yet not I, but the grace of God with me" (1 Corinthians 15:9-10).

Paul says there that his past made him the least of the apostles and even unfit to be called one. Yet that didn't paralyze him. He didn't sit in a corner and moan. Instead he entered into the present with zeal. Though last, he became first. He labored more than all of them. What mattered wasn't what he once was—"a persecutor of the church"—but what he became—"by the grace of God I am what I am." Whatever his past might have been, it was what he became by the grace of God that mattered.

Another way to make today your ally is to take advantage of the resources available in today. When painful memories come, don't worry with them. Concentrate instead on today—its beauty, its blessing, its opportunities for growth. Emphasize the positive emotions of faith, hope, love, laughter. Norman Cousins in his book *The Healing Heart* tells of visiting the Sepulveda, California, Veterans Administration Hospital. He encouraged the cancer patients there to develop some sort of ongoing program for creating an upbeat atmosphere among themselves. On returning to the hospital some weeks later he found that the most significant feature of their meetings was each person telling of something good that had happened to him since the last meeting. "They all contrived between meetings to make sure that they had some experience worth sharing with the others."[6] Counteract the pain of yesterday by counting the blessings of today.

Finally, use present memories to cancel out the old. Ian M. L. Hunter says that "the learning and retaining of current events can impede, interfere with, the retaining of past events."[7] That means your present can influence your past. Psychologists call this "retroactive interference." What you choose to remember of today can negate your painful memory of yesterday.

Is your painful memory one of guilt? Layer over that memory a new one of forgiveness. Is your painful memory one of loss? Build up memories of the gains and the good you have today. Is your painful memory one of being abused by another? Replace it with memories of Christ's love and of the love of the others in your life right now. Our memories are built to be selective. So be selective, but to the good side.

How to Heal Your Memories

Painful memories—they're there; they hurt; they bind us. What are we to do? Give in? Give up? Go crazy? When they come the future looks blank, black, empty with endless repe-

---

6. Norman Cousins, *The Healing Heart Antidotes to Panic and Helplessness* (New York: Norton, 1983), pp. 155-56.
7. Hunter, p. 258.

tition. And yet a possibility whispers itself. Possibly we can be healed, set free, changed.

But how?

How can something that has not been healed in fifteen, twenty-five, forty years be healed now? Here are some suggestions.

First, accept responsibility for your memories. Your painful memory may be of something that was done to you. Or it may be something you did. Either way it is your memory. It's part of you. And it's your responsibility. You don't have to approve of it. Only accept it. Face up to it. And quit trying to run away from it. Where can you go that it wouldn't be also?

Second, focus on now. Sufficient unto yesterday is its pain. Take advantage of the resources available to you today. When painful memories come, grab a broom and sweep the cobwebs from the ceiling. Play tennis. Figure out a complicated chess move. Do something to keep you from picking at the scab.

Third, choose the memories you want to embellish. Why should bad memories get all the attention? Why not invest some time in the good ones? Let your memory be selective in favor of memories of beauty, blessing, and grace. Keep the warm and satisfying. And discard the junk.

Fourth, release painful memories and experiences to God. Let them go. And let Him have them. Make a list of all the things that need to be healed. Make it as complete as you can. Then offer it all to the Father in prayer. Don't dictate how He should handle them. Just open them up to His touch, His love, His forgiveness.

Fifth, try a little holy imagination. Visualize again the event that has festered in your soul. Only this time as you run the video tape, superimpose Christ's presence onto the event. See Him walking back through time to those hidden moments. Visualize Him with you—loving you, supporting you, touching you, healing you, accepting you, forgiving you. Let His holy presence—which isn't a trick; He was really there when it happened—drive the bitterness and pain away.

Finally, accept His cleansing. Don't harbor the pain; turn from it. Be hardheaded. Satan enjoys seeing you hold on to rubbish. Refuse to let the enemy rake you over the coals again for something God has already dealt with. What God has cleansed, don't you call common.

6
A TIME TO SPEAK

Someone once quipped that the average number of times a man says no to temptation is once weakly.

It happened fifteen years ago—a little thing really. I walked into a bookstore, more to drool than to buy. And there it was—*the* book I wanted. Well, *a* book I wanted. I picked it up, mesmerized.

"Buy me," it whispered.

"I'd like to," I told it. "But I'd better not." I placed it back in the rack and moved on.

"Look at me," it said. "I'm just what you've wanted."

I stopped and looked back.

"I know," I said and took a half step toward it.

"You have the money in your pocket. Buy me."

"But I haven't asked Deborah yet."

"It's your money, isn't it? It's not needed for bills or any specific savings program, is it?"

"No, but..."

"Would you have hesitated before?"

"No."

"Am I expensive?"

"No."

"Buy me."

"But she might not approve. We've only been married a few weeks. I don't know what she would think."

"Don't tell her."

"But that's dishonest."

"It's better to say nothing than to take a chance on upsetting her. Come on, buy me."

Sweat began trickling down my forehead.

"It's no problem. Just sneak me home, read me on the sly, and stash me among your other books. Chances are she'll never notice."

"But..."

Light shimmered across its glossy cover.

"Buy me," it commanded.

I picked it up and headed to the cash register before better sense settled in.

It seems that the trivial things in life often have the greatest effects.

I took the book home with butterflies in my stomach. Deborah came home from work and kissed me. She trusts me, I thought ashamed. The book ceased to be a book then. It became instead a wall between us. I felt alienated, fragmented, alone. What kind of pattern was I setting for our marriage? It wasn't the item or its cost but the concealment that ate at me. The voice so feeble and small when I bought the book now roared and thundered. The choice was simple: stay quiet and stay alone or speak up, risk condemnation, and hope for forgiveness.

A Time for Honesty

We all reach a point sooner or later when we come face to face with ourselves, and we're not pleased with what we see. We knew all along that those nasty things were within us. But we were able to divert our attention elsewhere, using a mental sleight of hand to keep us from realizing the depths of our own depravity.

Then by God's sometimes severe grace we see ourselves unmasked, naked, covered with crud and corrosion of our own making. We can no longer hide behind all the old alibis—there are no circumstances left to blame; no others to accuse for misleading or bad advice; no grounds for claiming it's not our fault. Our sin is real sin; our wrong doing real evil.

At that point we can face the facts. Or we can put our masks back on in a futile attempt to hide from reality.

Facing facts—especially unpleasant facts—isn't easy. Something deep inside us cries out against such stark honesty. Yet face the facts we must, if we are to grow.

We need forgiveness. We need healing. We need restoring. Like the psalmist we could cry out: "Oh Lord, be gracious to me; heal my soul, for I have sinned against Thee" (Psalm 41:4).

Yet, how is that forgiveness to come?

It begins with confession—acknowledging how things really are—to ourselves, to God, and to the others we've hurt. Such confession is painful. It means giving up all the old masquerades, all the old evasions. It means admitting that we have sinned—the facts of it; our sorrow over it; and our desire to be forgiven. It means being willing to walk differently from now on.

One psychologist has said, "For him who confesses, shams are over and realities have begun; he has exteriorized his rottenness. If he has not actually got rid of it, he at least no longer smears it over with a hypocritical show of virtue—he lives at least upon a basis of veracity."[1]

Now is the time to begin realities. Today is the day for honesty. We can deny our sins and deceive only ourselves. Or we can confess our sins and be forgiven. (See 1 John 1:9.)

SILENCE IS NOT THE BEST POLICY

But what if we would rather not?

What if we would rather not "exteriorize our rottenness"? Doesn't acknowledging such things only make it worse? Can't we be restored and made whole without such exposure?

Psalm 32:3-4 provides an answer:

When I kept silent about my sin, my body wasted away
Through my groaning all day long.
For day and night Thy hand was heavy upon me;
My vitality was drained away as with the fever heat of summer.

Keeping silent about our sin destroys us. It's like swallowing poison. It eats away our insides. It dissolves our energy

---

1. William James, *The Varieties of Religious Experience* (New York: Longmans Green, 1929), pp. 462-63.

for living, our will to try. Emptiness consumes us until all that's left is a hollow shell, a whitewashed sepulcher.

The fact of secrecy is more important than the size of the offense. For me in the situation recounted at the beginning of the chapter it was buying a book when tight family finances demanded that even minor money decisions be shared. For David in our psalm it was adultery and murder. Yet the result was the same—spiritual disease, distress, depression, and despair.

Unfortunately, hidden sins are not self-limiting. They don't run their course and then disappear. Rather they have a strange immortality. Like the proverbial unwanted cat abandoned in the country only to show up the next day at home, hidden sins continue to chip away, eroding us into a pile of rubble.

On the one hand our nature cries for us to confess. On the other we cry that we cannot. What are we to do faced with the awful dilemma of to confess or not to confess?

All too often we follow the example of Adam and Eve:

> When the woman saw that the tree was good for food, and that it was a delight to the eyes, and that the tree was desirable to make one wise, she took from its fruit and ate; and she gave also to her husband with her, and he ate. Then the eyes of both of them were opened, and they knew that they were naked; and they sewed fig leaves together and made themselves loin coverings. And they heard the sound of the Lord God walking in the garden in the cool of the day, and the man and his wife hid themselves from the presence of the Lord God among the trees of the garden.
>
> (Genesis 3:6-8)

Commenting on that Scripture, John R. W. Stott said, "It is all very well smiling at their naivete; we too have our aprons of fig leaves, pathetic attempts to cover up, to conceal from God what we know ourselves to be."[2]

We want to conceal our sins even from ourselves. Acknowledging them is unbearable. We cannot stand the humiliation of seeing and facing ourselves as we really are. We may in our private prayer say we are sorry for our sins. But the words are hollow, the confession a formality. In them we cover more than we uncover.

---

2. John R. W. Stott, *Confess Your Sins* (Philadelphia: Westminster, 1965), p. 14.

Yet, however successful we may be in covering our sins from ourselves and others, we cannot conceal them from God. He knows us as we are, not as we want to think we are. All things are naked and open before Him. Hiding "from the presence of the Lord God among the trees of the garden" is ever a useless activity.

Proverbs 28:13 clearly states the alternative to hiding our sins, that is, confessing them. "He who conceals his transgressions will not prosper, but he who confesses and forsakes them will find compassion."

What does it mean?

It means that secrecy—covering, concealing, and masking sin—causes disintegration, spiritual poverty. And confession—honesty, openness, and self-disclosure—brings us mercy, spiritual prosperity. As one has said, "In keeping the matter private ... I still continue in my state of isolation. It is only with the help of confession that I am freed at last from the burden of moral exile."[3]

Who To Confess To

Yet, to whom am I to confess? God? The one or ones I've hurt? Some significant other?

The answer is another question: Whom have I sinned against? According to William Tyndale, "To whom a man trespasseth, unto him he ought to confess."

1. *Secret confession.* The first one to confess to is God. Dean Merrill says, "He is after all the one listener who will get it straight and not misinterpret us."[4] He is the one that will truly understand.

A more fundamental reason is that all sins are ultimately offenses against God.

Look at David in 2 Samuel 11-12. He saw Bathsheba bathing. He lusted after her, had her brought to him, and committed adultery with her. When he discovered she was pregnant, he connived to have her husband, Uriah, brought home from battle. David hoped to deceive Uriah into thinking the child was his. But Uriah, in loyalty to David and those still in battle against Rabbah, refused to lie with his wife. So

---

3. Carl G. Jung, *Modern Man in Search of a Soul* (New York: Harcourt Brace, 1933), p. 35.
4. Dean Merrill, *Another Chance: How God Overrides Our Big Mistakes* (Grand Rapids: Zondervan, 1981), p. 98.

David conspired with Joab to have Uriah murdered in battle.

In David's confession of those sins, he said, "Against Thee, Thee only, have I sinned, and done what is evil in Thy sight" (Psalm 51:4).

David wasn't trying to evade his responsibilities to Bathsheba, Uriah, or Joab. Nor was he denying that he had sinned against them. Rather he saw his sin as first and foremost against God. David recognized that, whatever his other responsibilities, he had first broken God's laws. He was admitting not merely that he had sinned but that he had sinned against God. He was not informing God of that—God already knew—but acknowledging to God the reality of his evil.

2. *Private confession.* Not all confession can begin and end with God however. All sins are against God, but some are against others as well. When our sin affects others, we must confess and seek their forgiveness too. The Bible emphasizes right relations with others, even teaching that we cannot draw near to God while estranged from another (Matthew 5:23-24). We must seek to repair the relationships we've damaged. We must muster the courage to talk to others as well as to God.

Oh, how we would prefer it otherwise. As Dean Merrill says, "We don't know whether our confession will be accepted or turned down; we fear an attack of blame instead of a welcoming spirit. In some cases we rationalize, 'What they don't know won't hurt them,' refusing all the while to admit that what they don't know is killing us, festering inside, poisoning all attempts at sincere dialogue. The days and weeks pass along in a haze of playacting; only a brave act of confession will clear the air."[5]

One way to make the task easier is to plan your words. Remember Jesus' story of the prodigal son? He planned his words: "I will get up and go to my father, and will say to him 'Father, I have sinned against heaven, and in your sight; I am no longer worthy to be called your son; make me as one of your hired men'" (Luke 15:18-19). Although he didn't get to finish all he'd planned to say, the words were important. They crystallized the about-face in his life.

Another way is to use common sense. Confess to others only those sins which directly affect them. For example, Jesus said that when a man looks on a woman in lust, he has

---

5. Ibid., p. 100.

already committed adultery (Matthew 5:28). But this adultery is in the sight of God and ought to be confessed to Him and not to her. Sins that have not erupted into word or deed ought to be confessed to God alone.

3. *Public confession.* When our sins are against a group of people—a community or a local congregation—we must confess to that group.

A biblical example of this is the story of Achan. Achan was a soldier in Joshua's army. But he disobeyed both Joshua's orders and God's by looting after the fall of Jericho. Because of his sin the army of Israel was defeated by the smaller army of Ai. When Achan's sin was discovered, Joshua called on him to make public confession (Joshua 7:19). Achan's sin was made known to all because all had suffered from his sin.

As with private confession, public confession must be tempered with common sense. Public confession that takes the form of bragging, or that magnifies details tempting to others, is hardly true confession.

THE THREE Rs

Earlier in this chapter we looked at Proverbs 28:13. Look at the last half of that verse again: "But he who confesses and forsakes them will find compassion." Up to this point we've focused on confession alone. But here God forges a link between confessing and forsaking.

What is the forsaking talked of here?

I believe it involves the three Rs: repentance, restitution, and restoration.

1. *Repentance.* Psychologist John Drakeford says that confession may be either positive or negative.[6] Negative confession is admitting our sin. Positive confession is following that admission up with remedial action.

Repentance is the hinge that swings negative confession into positive. It is the pivot that about-faces us from former fragmenting ways to new ways. According to Adin Steinsaltz, the Hebrew word for repentance has three different meanings. First, it means "return"—a going back to God. Second, it means "turning about" or "turning to"—adopting another orientation or direction in life. Finally, it means "response."[7]

6. John W. Drakeford, *Integrity Therapy* (Nashville: Broadman, 1967), p. 60. All rights reserved. Used by permission.
7. Adin Steinsaltz, "Repentance," *Parabola* (Winter 1983): 35.

In all three senses, repentance is a fundamental spiritual reality. We stumble over it, trying to hold onto pet sins and yet be forgiven them at the same time. But as with free lunches, there is not such a thing as an easy gospel or cheap grace.

Yet for all its severity, repentance, according to C. S. Lewis, "is not something God demands of you before He will take you back; . . . it is simply a description of what going back is like."

2. *Restitution.* Repairing our damaged relationships with others often involves restitution: paying them back for what we've taken; putting back something in the hole of their loss.

Restitution has a biblical pedigree. In the Old Testament Moses recorded:

> Then the Lord spoke to Moses, saying, "Speak to the sons of Israel, 'When a man or woman commits any of the sins of mankind, acting unfaithfully against the Lord, and that person is guilty, then he shall confess his sins which he has committed, and he shall make restitution in full for his wrong, and add to it one-fifth of it, and give it to him whom he has wronged.'"
>
> (Numbers 5:5-7)

Leviticus 6:1-7 records the same kind of commandment.

In the New Testament, the best example of restitution is Zaccheus (Luke 19:1-10). When Jesus came into his life, he resolved to live no longer on questionable taxing practices. Any money he'd gained by defrauding he promised to restore fourfold—a return of 400 percent rather than the 125 percent Moses commanded. Because some of those he'd defrauded could never be traced, Zaccheus proposed to give half of all his possessions to the poor. No wonder Jesus told him, "Today salvation has come to this house."

Many of us today are confused about restitution. How do we know when to do it and when not to?

The above Scriptures suggest that when we can, we must.

But what does restitution accomplish?

Perhaps it doesn't *accomplish* anything—at least not in the normal sense of the word. Restitution is not penance. It is not a means of atoning for our sin. It is not a method for making amends to God. Nor is it a technique for winning back God's favor. Restitution doesn't manipulate God at all.

But we should do it because our nature demands it. God doesn't need our restitution, we do. In restitution we show we really are made whole again. We demonstrate visibly to ourselves and to others just how much business we mean.

3. *Restoration.* What is restoration? Reunion with God. Old things wiped away; new things come. Our iniquity washed away. Our sin cleansed, removed, and forgotten. No more heart of stone. No more cold defiant spirit, but a heart of flesh, the Holy Spirit, and a new relationship.

Look at Joel 2. Sin brought punishment—a plague of locusts. Punishment brought repentance—a rending of hearts, not of garments. Repentance brought restoration:

> Then I will make up to you for the years
> That the swarming locust has eaten,
> The creeping locust, the stripping locust, and the gnawing locust.
> My great army which I sent among you.
>
> (Joel 2:25)

As Dean Merrill says, "It would be enough to gain relief from the pressures we brought upon ourselves. But to be repaid for lost time is almost unfathomable."[8]

Whether or not we feel forgiven and restored is inconsequential. Feelings don't matter. Facts do. It isn't the feeling, but the fact, that heals us.

GROUND RULES FOR CONFESSION[9]

First, make confession specific. It costs nothing for us to admit, "I'm not what I ought to be." It costs no more to say, "I ought to be a better Christian." But it costs a great deal to be honest and say, "I've been a troublemaker in this church," or, "I've been bitterly jealous of _____ and have slandered him to others." Sin is specific and ought to be confessed specifically.

Second, make confession promptly. The best time to confess is when conviction comes. Don't wait. Don't put it off. Think of it in terms of a sign that showed up at a drive-in carwash: "Regular washing pays off." Just like an auto's paint and chrome, we need continual cleansing to keep our lives bright and useful.

Third, make confession thorough. Begin with that besetting

---

8. Merrill, p. 103.
9. I'm indebted to John W. Drakeford for the insight in the sixth, seventh, and eighth suggestions made here.

sin—the one you feel the most conviction over. Keep going until there's nothing left to confess.

Fourth, don't try to make excuses. We did what we did when we did it. All the extenuating circumstances we manufacture won't alter that. Abandon hypocrisy.

Fifth, remember that the goal of confession is not emotional release but spiritual healing. The purpose of confession is not to feel better—although you will—but to be made whole again. Confession is not a "numbzit" for our consciences, but a curing of spiritual disease.

Sixth, remember too that confession is not complaining. Complaining focuses on emotions. With true confession the issue isn't "I feel bad about it" but "I did wrong." Confession isn't a bath of self-pity but an acknowledgement of irresponsibility.

Seventh, don't use confession as a tool for blaming others. A woman decides to confess an act of unfaithfulness to her husband. But she "confesses" in such a way as to make it his fault—"If you had been more attentive, it wouldn't have happened!"

Eighth, confess for yourself and not for others. Confess what you did, not what someone else did to tempt you. Accept the responsibility that is rightly yours, and let God deal with others on theirs.

Finally, be willing to accept the judgment of others. Sometimes we fear that if we open ourselves and acknowledge our sins, others will not understand. The one we confess to may look down on us in contempt. The danger is real. Although God has already declared His love and forgiveness, the others we've hurt may not be so merciful. Face that fear. And face their judgment. It is the only way to win through.

7

A Time to Listen

Pararadox. On the one hand God's voice is the last thing we want to hear. After all, the thought goes, if He'd made us better, or done a better job managing things, we wouldn't be in this fix. On the other hand, we want desperately to hear Him speak. We think that if we could catch some word from Him things would be better.

So we're caught in a paradox, wanting and not wanting, afraid He will and afraid He won't, and wondering if it's all worth it anyway.

The Flip Side of Prayer

A Bible teacher I respect greatly says that God answers prayer in one of three ways: yes, no, or wait awhile.

That's good as far as it goes. However, some of our requests require more elaboration than a simple yes, no, or wait provides. Questions like: Where do I go from here? What do You want me to do next? How can I climb this mountain?

That's where listening comes in. It's the flip side of prayer. Yet, how do you hear His voice? How do you listen to God?

Listening isn't easy. Think how hard it is to listen to people whose voices we can hear. The hostess of a women's group decided to test how well the group listened. She took a tray of goodies and said to each guest, "Do try one. I've filled them all with strychnine." No one hesitated. "Lovely," each replied. "I must have your recipe."

A pastor and his wife stood greeting church members after the service. The pastor's mind still floated somewhere with his sermon. Suddenly he came back to himself and realized that he hadn't heard a word the man before him had spoken. He swallowed once and decided to bluff it. The word *vacation* fluttered into his awareness.

"Sounds like you had a great time," he said.

The man glared at him and without another word hobbled off on crutches.

The minister's wife, scarlet faced, whispered to her husband, "He just told you how he'd had an accident, broke his leg, and spent four days in the hospital."

We listen, but we don't hear. In that empty moment when our mouths are shut, our minds are yet in full gear, worlds away from the words directed our way.

Begin by Stilling the Inner Hubbub

Learning to hear His voice begins with stilling the inner hubbub.

At times—especially when we feel we're about to sink—we all carry within ourselves a cacophonic symphony, a discordant melody of helter-skelter impulses, jumbled desires, and tumultous cares. The bellow of that inner clamor annihilates the meaning of any outside voice.

One summer my Cub Scout den mother owned a share in a co-op swimming pool. Naturally, all our meetings took place at the pool. I was great at water play but poor to worse at swimming. Insecurity and inability both demanded that I stand every few minutes, my head safely out of the water, my feet secured to the bottom of the pool.

During one of our meetings, I stopped to stand and abruptly discovered I was in the deep end. I panicked and began to struggle. Across the pool my cousin yelled that I needed help. The lifeguard answered, "No, he's just playing."

The den mother stood talking to another adult. And all about me twenty other boys splashed and yelled.

I didn't hear any of it. My world was limited to the screams in my head, the roar in my ears, and the pain in my lungs. I didn't hear my cousin slicing through the water trying to reach me, nor the splash of the lifeguard, who suddenly decided I wasn't playing. My inner clamor was too great.

Strong hands reached me and lifted me from the water. I knew dimly that I was on the side of the pool, with someone pumping the water from me. Only then did I hear the voices of concerned people all around me.

Listening begins with stilling the inner hubbub, quieting the panic, and opening our ears to the sound of redemption drawing nigh.

Look to Where His Voice Is Heard

THE VOICE OF OTHERS

In the wilderness Moses sat to judge the people as they gathered around him from morning to evening. When Moses' father-in-law saw what was going on, he said to Moses, "The thing that you are doing is not good. You will surely wear out, both yourself and these people who are with you, for the task is too heavy for you; you cannot do it alone" (Exodus 18:17-18). Then he counseled Moses on a better way to handle the problem.

Sometimes God speaks through the voice of others. He speaks through books, ministers, mates, friends, godly acquaintances, parents, and children.

In one of his sermons George W. Truett told of a young man whose beautiful wife died after an extremely short illness. The man was left with a little four-or-five-year-old girl. That evening at home the child cried for her mother long into the night. The father petted and comforted her as best he could. Finally, out of sorrow for her father, the little girl stopped sobbing.

All was silent for a time. Then in the blackness the father whispered, "God, I trust you; but, oh, it's as dark as midnight."

At that the little girl started crying again. And her father said, "I thought you were asleep, baby."

"I tried, Daddy," she answered. "I was sorry for you. I did try; but I couldn't go to sleep." She paused. "Daddy, did you ever know it to be so dark? I can't even see you." She started crying again. "But, Daddy, you love me even if it's dark, don't you? You love me even if I don't see you, don't you?"

The father reached out with big hands, took up his little girl, and mothered her until at last she went to sleep.

Then he took her cry and passed it upward. "Father, it's dark as midnight. And I can't see You at all. But You love me even if it's dark, don't You? You love me even if I can't see You, don't You?"

And then, according to Truett, "the darkness was like unto day."[1]

EVENTS

We are all familiar with the open door/closed door approach. Paul ran into it in Acts 16:6-10, when the door to Bithynia was closed because God wanted him in Macedonia.

Several years ago a young man fresh out of seminary was torn between what appeared to him to be two mutually exclusive ministries. Unable to determine which to focus on, he tried both. Two years passed, and he began to realize something. One ministry had tapered off; fewer and fewer opportunities came. The other, quite without effort on his part, had grown. Through open door/closed door events he had his answer.

Abrupt changes in circumstance, near catastrophes, and absolute disasters can carry the voice of God. This is not to say that God causes all these things but that through them He can yet speak. Remember Romans 8:28—"And we know that God causes all things to work together for good to those who love God, to those who are called according to His purpose."

OUR OWN CONTEMPLATION AND REASONING

Resistance usually sets in at this point. How often we presuppose that wisdom and reasoning—even in a believer—are so utterly defective as to be totally useless. This prejudice against contemplation and reasoning ignores the fact that a brain and the ability to use it are as much a part of how God made us as a right and left hand.

Second Timothy 1:7 in the King James Version says, "God hath not given us the spirit of fear; but of power, and of love, and of a sound mind."

What is meant by "a sound mind" that it should be a part of God's blueprint for a believer? It doesn't mean that God

1. George W. Truett, "What to Do with Life's Burdens," *A Quest for Souls* (Grand Rapids: Eerdmans, 1917; reprint ed., 1966), pp. 24-26. Used by permission.

makes every believer a candidate for Mensa, the international high IQ society. It does mean that God provides a believer with all that's necessary for trustworthy thinking.

Remember these three don'ts.

Don't trust worldly wisdom. What the world calls smart, God often calls stupid.

Don't forget to ask for spiritual wisdom. James 1:5 says, "But if any of you lacks wisdom, let him ask of God, who gives to all men generously and without reproach, and it will be given to him."

And don't ignore the fruit of a sound remade mind. The wisdom of man is indeed lower than God's foolishness, but it is considerably higher than man's foolishness. Don't be afraid to mull over a problem, issue, or question, and then let sanctified reasoning suggest an answer.

THE STILL SMALL VOICE

Elijah knew the problems of spiritual survival. On Mt. Carmel he stood alone against 450 prophets of Baal. A few days later under a juniper tree in the wilderness, he asked to die.

Eventually he found himself in a cave on Mt. Horeb. God said, "Go forth, and stand on the mountain." Elijah went and discovered that the Lord was passing by.

A great and strong wind came, rending the mountains and breaking rocks in pieces. But God wasn't in the wind. An earthquake came. But the Lord wasn't in the earthquake. Then a fire roared. But God wasn't in the fire either. Finally, a gentle blowing came, and in it God spoke (I Kings 19:11-13).

Sometimes God speaks with a still, small voice. He confronts us with a quality of rightness that, quite apart from reason, can't be denied.

SCRIPTURE

We've known that God speaks through Scripture from our youth up. Yet, *how* does He speak through Scripture? Or, more to the point, does He address every issue?

Yes and no. No in the sense that there are no verses telling us specifically whom to marry, what job to seek, where to live, or what to do next when disaster overwhelms us. Can you imagine the size of Bible needed to carry such individualized instruction for every person that has and will ever live?

The answer is yes, though, in the things that are covered: injunctions not to fear (this occurs over seventy times), exhortations to trust and believe, appeals to obey. These are the principles that give our lives shape, just as a skeleton gives the body shape.

We are not told whom to marry. But we are told what kind of mate to seek. We are to seek someone who is a believer (2 Corinthians 6:14), someone chaste (1 Peter 3:2), someone virtuous (Proverbs 12:4), and someone we can love (Colossians 3:19, Titus 2:4). In a husband look for someone you can submit to (Colossians 3:18) and someone who is or can be a provider (1 Timothy 5:8). In a wife look for someone you can honor (1 Peter 3:7), someone with wisdom (Proverbs 14:1), someone with prudence (Proverbs 19:14), and someone strongly lacking in contentiousness (Proverbs 21:9).

Block Out the False Voices

Unfortunately, each of these avenues of God's voice can also be used by Satan. Learn to discern the false voices.

Others, even godly others, can give bad advice.

Open and closed doors are likewise untrustworthy. Not every door is right. There was a ship ready to sail. Space was available. He had money for the ticket. And the captain was willing to sell him passage. But, for Jonah, Tarshish was the wrong decision.

Unredeemed reason overflows with false, malicious, life-ruining thoughts. Even redeemed reason can be warped by duress. Aaron, feeling the strain of Moses' long absence, capitulated to an angry mob and made for them the golden calf (Exodus 32:1-6).

Whose small voice is it? What is it urging us to do? A guest brought an uninvited acquaintance to his host's for dinner. "God told me to do it," he said. "I think not," his hostess replied, "for God is a gentleman." Who is right? Who is wrong?

Even Scripture can be used falsely. A verse taken out of context resulted in one little boy's being told, "God doesn't want you" (Hebrews 6:6). Satan took Jesus from the wilderness into Jerusalem and stood Him on the pinnacle of the Temple. There he tempted Christ with Scripture (Matthew 4:5-6).

How then do you know which voice is true and which is false?

Look for a lining up. God won't necessarily use all five of these, but He won't contradict Himself either. Only Scripture—taken in context and in light of its whole—can stand alone. Look for the others to line up with it. Then when people, events, reasoning, and inner oughtness agree with biblical principles, go for it.

Listen with Your Whole Self

What does it mean to listen with the whole self? It means we don't block out what we hear. Sometimes we just don't want to hear what He has to say. Then, just as a photographer uses filters to shut out unwanted light, we use our emotions to filter out what we're unwilling to hear. We sift out the negative, the things we don't want to be confronted with, as if we could actually prosper by hiding from the don'ts, the dos, and the disciplines of life. So we hesitate, avoid, and try to look inconspicuous, as if any of that does anything but hurt.

Listening with the whole self means listening with hope. We know that the greatest is love; but we forget that the runner up is hope. Hope in what? Not hope that we'll get what we want, but that we'll get something better. Hope for deliverance. Hope that says it won't always be this way. Hope for a brighter tomorrow.

It also means listening with trust. Too often in my depressions I've tried to console myself with the words "I'm tired and I'm lonely." But those are cold words, with no security. And they set up a spiral of despair, driving me ever deeper.

I've discovered that better words for such moments are "I am loved." Me. Larry E. Neagle. God is not out to get me. Nor am I just a passing interest, receiving only partial attention. He loves me. He said so on a cross.

And He loves you. Yes, you. Wherever you go, He is—ahead of you, behind you, above you, below you, in you. And wherever He is, love is. Personal love. His for you. Listen and trust.

8
CULTIVATING FAITHFULNESS

Someone once said that "faith is, at one and the same time, absolutely necessary and altogether impossible." It is absolutely necessary, for "without faith it is impossible to please Him" (Hebrews 11:6). And it is altogether impossible because in ourselves we have no means of doing that which is good, acceptable, and right (see Romans 3).

What are we then to do? If faith is the currency of spiritual commerce, how are we to survive when we're destitute? How can we increase our supply? How can we have more faith?

"Everyone says I should have more faith, but no one tells me how to get it."

"I've tried and tried, but nothing seems to work. Why isn't my faith stronger?"

"Until this happened things were OK. Now I think I'm losing my faith. What can I do? How can I halt it?"

In spiritual survival, faith seems to be as big a problem as sin and guilt. But is faith really the problem? Or is it doubt?

CONFESSIONS OF A HABITUAL DOUBTER

Let me introduce you to a habitual doubter: me. It's not

easy to admit to, and perhaps I overdo it. Yet in most faith crises I instinctively follow in the path of the apostle Thomas. I doubt.

Why do I doubt? Most often I doubt because I'm afraid. I'm afraid my beliefs may be false. Maybe they're wish-fulfillment. If I face them head-on I might discover that and be disappointed. Sometimes I'm afraid my beliefs might be true. The French philosopher Pascal asked, "Why is it so hard to believe?" He answered by saying, "Because it is so hard to obey." Doubting saves me embarrassment, nuisance, and inconvenience.

Sometimes I doubt because it's easy. I tell myself it's only natural to leave my bridges unburned. Faith is so hard. And I may be wrong. It's easier to hide in doubt. After all, doubt is logical. Doubt is safe. Doubt doesn't risk anything. Doubt doesn't lead me any place dangerous—any place where I may be inadequate, inept, mistaken.

Sometimes I doubt because of frustrations and disappointments. Things happen beyond my control. Things I don't want. Things that hurt. I feel impotent. Helpless. And I doubt.

Sometimes I doubt because I'm overwhelmed by my own sin. I am swamped with a sense of my own limitations. Part of me seeks God. Part of me flees the other way. I want to reach out. But a feeling that—in spite of all that God has said and done—He really doesn't care about me engulfs me. He has a few favorites on whom He sends sunshine, I tell myself. And I'm not one of them.

Sometimes I doubt intellectually. Things happen that I don't understand. And I feel compelled to search for rational explanations, facts, visible proof. I forget that we are to "walk by faith, not by sight" (2 Corinthians 5:7). I would rather reverse it. After all, seeing is believing, isn't it? I forget that proof is a rebellion against reality. It doesn't always exist. Facts can be interpreted any number of ways. And explanations are not owed to me.

Sometimes I doubt because of my emotions. My mind does not always work reasonably. Years ago an acquaintance took me up for my first flight in a small airplane. Within minutes I found myself clutching the seat, expecting the thin metal beneath me to rip away and let me plummet to the ground. The more I told myself it wasn't logical, the harder I clasped the seat. My problem wasn't faith versus reason but faith and reason versus emotions and desires.

Sometimes I doubt because of out-of-kilter personal relationships. The way I think and feel about someone close often gets tied up in how I think and feel about God. Problems with one easily extend to problems with the other. A sour, unsatisfying, insecure relationship with anyone important to me leaves me feeling alone and alienated even from God.

Sometimes I doubt because of the nature of faith itself. Some think that faith ignores fact. It doesn't. Faith does go beyond fact, beyond the obvious truths that anyone can immediately perceive. We do not see or hear God the way we see or hear an orchestra play a symphony. Can we really "prove" life after death or answered prayer? Faith addresses realities not so easily grasped. Then too, faith is so vulnerable. It's like betting everything you have on one throw of the dice, one hand of cards, one sweepstakes ticket. Doubt seems so much safer than faith.

But is it?

Is Doubt Ever Beneficial?

Only sometimes. Sometimes doubt stimulates growth. When doubt is faced honestly and openly, it can be a goad to faith. We are forced then to choose answers to deep and perplexing questions. When we choose aright, faith increases. It was not without reason that so many of God's servants spent time in the wilderness.

Most of the time, however, doubt works against us. Part of the problem is our own response to doubt. We can hold it at arm's length and free ourselves to deal with it. Or we can embrace it. Surrender to it. Get drunk on it, and lose. Our choice determines doubt's strength.

An old proverb says, "Feed your faith and faith will grow, feed your doubt and doubt will grow." Contrary to what some have said, the two do work against each other. Feeding one starves the other. When doubt takes over, faith suffers.

What happens when we doubt?

Doubt tempts us to quit. The stronger our faith, the more we try. The stronger our doubts, the more we want to give up. Doubt locks us up inside ourselves. It imprisons us in a dungeon of disbelief. It chains us to panic and helplessness. It starves away our energy and leaves us powerless. For that reason, a doubting person—a faith-less person—is always less of a person than he might otherwise be.

Doubt leaves us helpless. James 1:6-8 says, "The one who doubts is like the surf of the sea driven and tossed by the wind. For let not that man expect that he will receive anything from the Lord, being a double-minded man, unstable in all his ways." Doubt takes us out into a stormy sea. It ties our hands and encases our feet. It destroys our rudder, tatters our sails, and laughs as the storm overwhelms us. Sundered from God's stability, we frantically call out to anything or anyone that might offer us help—only to find each new "savior" as sea driven as ourselves.

Doubt destroys hope and makes men die. During World War II, Viktor Frankl spent years in a Nazi concentration camp. Later he wrote, "The prisoner who had lost his faith in the future—his future—was doomed. With his loss of belief in the future, he also lost his spiritual hold; he let himself decline and become subject to mental and physical decay."[1] Faith, Frankl saw, enabled men to survive. Doubt led them to give up and die.

Doubt's worst effect isn't just death to the doubter. Seen from a different angle, doubt is little more than a polite way of spiritual rebellion. It's a genteel way of saying to God, "We believe You, and we don't believe You. Mostly we don't. That is, we believe You're going to take care of us, get us through this time of pain . . . maybe . . . if You will." First John 5:10 says, "The one who does not believe God has made Him a liar." We do not often see our doubts in this light. Yet the truth is that doubt, or disbelief, maligns God's truthfulness and defames His character.

What Is Faith?

Definitions are a good place to begin. Scripture uses the word in several different ways. Sometimes it uses faith in the sense of belief—"O men of little faith" (Matthew 6:30). Sometimes it uses faith in the sense of trust—"Have faith in God" (Mark 11:22). Sometimes it uses faith in the sense of Christianity as a whole—"Test yourselves to see if you are in the faith" (2 Corinthians 13:5). Sometimes it means a combination of any or all three—"I have fought the good fight, I have finished the course, I have kept the faith" (2 Timothy 4:7).

Hannah W. Smith in her classic book *The Christian's Secret*

---

1. Viktor E. Frankl, *Man's Search for Meaning* (New York: Simon & Schuster, 1985), p. 85.

of a Happy Life says that faith "is nothing more nor less than just believing God when He says He either has done something for us, or will do it; and then trusting Him to keep His word."[2]

WHAT FAITH IS

- Faith is commitment.
- Faith is singlemindedness.
- Faith is assent.
- Faith is attitude.
- Faith is action.

Attitudes always reflect themselves in actions. Belief always influences behavior. It is reliance on God and obedience to God. Faith is the response of a person to a person.

"Now faith is the assurance of things hoped for, the conviction of things not seen" (Hebrews 11:1).

WHAT FAITH IS NOT

Faith is not just believing. Faith's value lies not in the believing but in what you believe. You can believe anything. If what you believe is true, you benefit. If what you believe is false, you lose. In both cases believing is the same, only the objects of that belief vary. As important as believing is, it is insufficient on its own. After all, "the demons also believe, and shudder" (James 2:19*b*).

Faith is not merely believing in a set of principles. Faith isn't like trigonometry where you believe a table of logarithms is correct—you never use them, so you never have reason to doubt them. Faith isn't just an opinion about things. It isn't a theological theory; it's a way of life. It isn't an interpretation of God; it's a way to experience God. Faith opens the door that lets God into one's life.

Faith is not fantasy or wishful thinking. Faith does not disregard reality; it embraces it. If your arm is broken, your pantry empty, your bank account depleted, there is no value in pretending otherwise. Pretending your arm is healed, your pantry full, and your bank account prosperous changes nothing. Pretense is dishonest, and God is truth.

---

2. Hannah Whitall Smith, *The Christian's Secret of a Happy Life* (Old Tappan, N.J.: Revell, 1961), p. 71.

Finally, faith is not coercing God. We want things and think that if only we had faith He would grant them to us. Too often we are like the old man who read in his Bible, "If you have faith as a mustard seed, you shall say to this mountain, 'Move from here to there,' and it shall move" (Matthew 17:20). There was no mountain nearby; but there was a small hill that stood between his home and the village. That hill was an increasing source of weariness to his aging limbs. So he prayed one night for it to be removed. His prayer done, he flung open the door. And there was the hill in the same old place. He stared at it in disgust and said, "Humph, just as I expected!" That old man saw faith as a way of manipulating God into letting him have his own way.

A TIME TO CHOOSE

Psalm 37:3 says, "Trust in the Lord, and do good; dwell in the land and cultivate faithfulness."

Cultivate faithfulness: Is such a thing possible? What is our own role in the establishment of our faith?

The answer is *choosing*. Near the end of Moses' life, not long before the children of Israel were to enter the promised land, God again made a covenant with the people in the land of Moab. Near the end of that covenant God told them to choose: "I call heaven and earth to witness against you today, that I have set before you life and death, the blessing and the curse. So choose life in order that you may live, you and your descendants" (Deuteronomy 30:19). Likewise, Joshua, in the farewell address of his ministry, said, "Choose for yourselves today whom you will serve" (Joshua 24:15*b*).

Choosing is still our responsibility and our freedom. We began the Christian life by choosing to believe that Jesus is the Son of God and trusting Him to do what we cannot—make us right with God. So in the life that follows, we must choose: choose faith and believe; choose doubt and disbelieve.

In *The Last Battle*, by C. S. Lewis, a group of human followers of the great lion Aslan (who portrays Jesus) are cast into a small thatched stable. Although they don't know it yet, they died coming through the stable door. In the stable are a dozen dwarfs—also unknowingly dead. For the humans the inside of the stable is a new world—the real Narnia. For the dwarfs the inside of the stable is a dark filthy prison. The humans try to convince the dwarfs—who were once themselves followers of Aslan—to come out and enjoy the bright

Narnian day. The dwarfs refuse. They feel betrayed by Aslan and will no longer believe.

Then Aslan comes. When his followers ask him to do something about the dwarfs, Aslan says, "I will show you both what I can, and what I cannot, do." Aslan gives a low growl. But the dwarfs think it comes from a false Aslan. Aslan shakes his mane causing a feast to appear on each dwarf's knee. The feast, however, seems to the dwarfs as only the kind of food one might find in a stable. They eat, drink, fight, and chant, "We haven't let anyone take us in. The dwarfs are for the dwarfs."

Aslan turns to the others and says, "You see, they will not let us help them. They have chosen cunning instead of belief. Their prison is only in their own minds, yet they are in that prison; and so afraid of being taken in that they cannot be taken out."[3]

The dwarfs had chosen not to believe. Just so we can will *to* believe.

Does that sound all one-sided—saying that we believe because we will to? Does it sound too human, too much of our own efforts?

Paul answered that: "For it is God who is at work in you, both to will and to work for His good pleasure" (Philippians 2:13). In willing to believe, God's will precedes ours. Our willingness is merely a response to His. C. S. Lewis in *The Great Divorce* says, "There are only two kinds of people in the end: those who say to God, 'Thy will be done,' and those to whom God says, in the end, 'Thy will be done.' "[4] God's grace makes possible the otherwise impossible—faith, and the ability to say, "Thy will be done."

STEPPING OUT

Earlier I said that faith is both attitude and action, belief and behavior. That is the *do* part Paul mentioned in the verse above.

But how does one *do* faith? By acting on belief and trust.

Acting on faith isn't easy. Even when our belief and trust are firmly founded within us, we often find ourselves stymied at behaving it out. The problem is compounded when our belief and trust are not so firmly seated. Our emotions and

---

3. C. S. Lewis, *The Last Battle* (New York: Macmillan, 1956), pp. 128-40.
4. C. S. Lewis, *The Great Divorce* (New York: Macmillan, 1946), p. 73.

circumstances come then and shout, "Doubt! Disbelieve! You'll just be a hypocrite if you try to act out something you don't feel."

What are we to do then? Choosing to act with faith in a situation not because we feel it or see it, but because He said it, is hard beyond degree. How do we act out faith when bad news comes, when we're in trouble, when others around us laugh at us, and all our emotions rise up in a blitz on belief? How can we choose to go against all our senses and desires and act on something that seems absolutely untrue? Such self-denial seems beyond us.

But it isn't.

We can nonetheless act as if we believed. When our lives cave in, we can act as if we believed "that God causes all things to work together for good to those who love God, to those who are called according to His purpose" (Romans 8:28). When our plans turn sour, we can act as if we really believed that "He who promised is faithful" (Hebrews 10:23). When we're naked and hungry, we can act as if we believed "Seek first His kingdom and His righteousness; and all these things shall be added to you" (Matthew 6:33).

And in the doing a strange thing occurs. We find the assurance of faith our mind sought for in the proof of our own experience. Jesus said, "If any man is willing to do His will, he shall know of the teaching, whether it is of God, or whether I speak from Myself" (John 7:17). Knowing comes from doing.

How to Cultivate Faithfulness

First, start where you are. Don't worry that you don't have ten talents of faith like someone else. Stop berating yourself for what you don't have. Start with the faith you do have. Invest it. Plant it. Act upon it. It will grow.

Second, begin with honesty. Honesty with God and with oneself is the beginning place for any act of spiritual survival. Don't play games trying to hide what cannot be hidden. Face the truth. Don't run from it; walk toward it. Faith grows from reality, not fantasy. It embraces what is, not what we wish was.

Third, learn to deal with shifting moods. C. S. Lewis once defined faith as "the art of holding on to things your reason has once accepted, in spite of your changing moods."[5] In the

---

5. C. S. Lewis, *Mere Christianity* (New York: Macmillan, 1952).

New Testament the word *faith* appears 234 times, the word *believe* 251 times—they come from the same root word. Yet the word *feel* appears only five times and not in the context of telling us how to live. Stop considering your emotions. Make faith rule over them, not them over faith.

Fourth, make faith your goal. The power of goal setting is well known. A business sets a sales goal and reaches it. A church sets a membership goal and reaches it. A writer sets a words-per-day goal and reaches it. Make faith your goal. Make your goals statements of faith.

Fifth, feed your faith. It will not automatically remain strong. It must be fed. How can you feed it? By daily prayer, devotional reading, and regular church attendance. We cannot deepen faith unless we make contact with it. We need reminding of what we believe. We need the anchoring of other believers. Shorn of that double stability, we drift at the mercy of the tide in the face of a coming storm.

Sixth, choose your thoughts. Paul wrote, "Finally, brethren, whatever is true, whatever is honorable, whatever is right, whatever is pure, whatever is lovely, whatever is of good repute, if there is any excellence and if anything worthy of praise, let your mind dwell on these things" (Philippians 4:8). Why think negative, crippling, paralyzing thoughts, when you can think positive, emancipating, empowering ones? Abandon the gospel of St. Murphy, and embrace the gospel of Jesus Christ. Quit focusing your thinking on doubt, pain, weakness, poverty, failure, hatefulness, alienation, loneliness, envy, lust, and dishonor. Focus instead on God who has peace, strength, abundance, success, kindness, affection, friendship, generosity, purity, and honor.

Seventh, behave accordingly. Don't be a dilettante—a dabbler, a piddler, a trifler. G. K. Chesterton once observed, "The Christian ideal has not been tried and found wanting; it has been found difficult and left untried." We need to relearn the meaning of a forgotten word in Scripture: diligence. Real faith is always heroic. Real faith is singleminded. Real faith makes dedicated effort.

Finally, be patient. There are no spiritual shortcuts to faith. Relax. Don't tie yourself in spiritual knots. Ease up on yourself. Give God time to work a quality product.

9
COMFORTING WITH THE COMFORT WE'VE RECEIVED

A frustrating day. Bills were heaped up in the middle of my desk. My work car wouldn't start. And I was approaching a deadline unprepared.

It looked like an opportune time for depression.

Then in popped my middle daughter with a shy smile. "Here, Daddy. This is for you. Read it, OK?"

It was a small booklet, handmade from manila drawing paper. On the outside it read, "Daddy's Secret Book, by Tara." Inside were drawings of different things we had done together recently—hugging, allowances, doing the dishes. Near the end she had printed in her best eight-year-old's hand, "Dear Dad: I love you a lot—very, very, very much. Love, Tara."

COMFORT AND SPIRITUAL SURVIVAL

Have you ever needed a similar message?

We all have times when we desperately need a helping hand, an act of love, a hug of comfort. We all at times need the candle of someone else's care to penetrate the darkness surrounding us. Part of spiritual survival is locating comfort, accepting it, and growing by it.

But an equal part is sharing the comfort we've received with others.

Consider 2 Corinthians 1:3-4.

> Blessed be the God and Father of our Lord Jesus Christ, the Father of mercies and God of all comfort; who comforts us in all our affliction so that we may be able to comfort those who are in any affliction with the comfort with which we ourselves are comforted by God.

Comforting with the comfort we've received, caring as we've been cared for—it's an imposing thought, isn't it? All the more so when we feel we've not been properly comforted or cared for. What kind of comfort can we offer when our own coffers are bare? What kind of care can we give when no one cares for us?

It seems ridiculous when we're in the deep water to reach out to others who are drowning. We ourselves have only just begun to learn how to stay afloat. We have so little to offer yet—precarious strength, unpracticed technique, questionable abilities. If we grab hold, we both may drown. How easy it is to say, "Wait until I'm stronger, more practiced, more able." And then struggle past them as we suppose others to have struggled past us.

Yet, contrary to logic, part of survival is reaching out to others. It's a paradox. If you want to save your life, lose it. If you want to have, give. If you want to survive, comfort others.

Remember the 1950s? We called that decade the Silent Generation. Then came the 1960s, the Now Generation. And the 1970s we dubbed the Me Generation. The progression has born its logical fruit—the 1980s are what one sociologist calls the Uncaring Generation.[1]

Why uncaring? The contention is that we care so much for ourselves that there's no room for others. The tide of self has risen to a flood of self-help, self-seeking, self-fulfillment. The result? As another sociologist says, we have become hollow.[2]

1. Donald H. Bouma, "Caring in an Uncaring Society," *USA Today* (May 1983):19.
2. Amitai Etzioni, *An Immodest Agenda: Rebuilding America Before the 21st Century* (New York: McGraw-Hill, 1982).

In seeking to fill ourselves, we emptied ourselves. In seeking self-growth, we've shrunk.

In this book we've focused primarily on self-skills: handling tragedy, guilt, failure, painful memories, and—in the next chapter—burnout. It's time—even in the midst of our own struggles—to remember our connections. It's time to reach out, to unhollow, to tend to the needs of others.

Lewis Thomas, M.D. and essayist, says that caring is based on kinship.[3] We care for those we consider family. We care for those with whom we feel affinity. Look around. All the world is drowning, and we have spiritual kin in need. We are still our brother's keepers.

Reaching Out to Others

In his book *Joy Comes with the Morning* William Kinnaird says that by indifference we invite people to die.[4]

Frightening, isn't it?

Our indifference—our apathy, disinterest, unconcern, nonchalance—says to others, "Bug off. You're unimportant. You're irrelevant. You're trivial. You're mediocre. Why don't you go somewhere out of my way, permanently."

Have you recently invited someone to die? Has someone recently invited you?

We could define comfort as inviting others to live. The word comes from a Latin word meaning "to strengthen." The way we use it today, it means that and more: to give hope, to cheer, to soothe, to console, to encourage.

Perhaps that last word says it best: encourage. The world is full of discouragement—put-downs, ridicules, invitations to die. It's so easy to wonder *what's the use?* and quit. We all need encouragers.

I used to keep a small garden in my back yard. I never followed all the rules, so it never amounted to all it could have. So it is with people. As gardens we need a gardener to help us grow. But we don't need just any gardener. We don't need a lazy gardener—one who will let us wilt and die daily for lack of care. We need a loving gardener—one who helps us flourish by tender care. We need encouragers; and we need to encourage.

3. Lewis Thomas, "Altruism: Self-Sacrifice for Others," *Saturday Evening Post* (May/June 1982):44.
4. William M. Kinnaird, *Joy Comes with the Morning* (Waco, Tex.: Word, 1979), p. 53.

Sarah is an apparently successful working wife. She has a good job as a computer programmer and makes a good salary. Yet she faces each day frustrated and afraid. She feels inadequate for her job. She's convinced that in a short time her lack will become obvious, and she will crumble.

Jim works three jobs trying to support his family of five. And there just isn't enough to go around. Each new need is met with bitterness and anger. He feels pressured, misunderstood, and impotent. He isn't pleasant to be with, and he knows it. But he doesn't seem to be able to do anything about it. Oh, he knows he won't go under—he's faced worse and survived. But that doesn't stop the stress or the pain.

Both Sarah and Jim need someone to listen, someone to understand, someone to comfort and encourage.

BEGIN WITH JERUSALEM

In the book of Acts Jesus gives His marching orders to the church:

> But you shall receive power when the Holy Spirit has come upon you; and you shall be My witnesses both in Jerusalem, and in all Judea and Samaria, and even to the remotest part of the earth. (Acts 1:8) □

Think of it in terms of concentric circles. Begin at Jerusalem—begin at home—and work your way out to your extended family, your neighborhood, all the world. Comfort works in just such a fashion.

Reach out to your family. Have you ever noticed how many times the New Testament, from Acts on, refers to the church in someone's house? Mission-minded people have based the concept of house churches on those references. Perhaps there's another truth there as well. The church in your home is not just the church that meets there. It's also the church that lives there. God intends for dads to be the corporeal leaders of that church. Moms are the assistant leaders and—if the dads cop out—their replacements. Kids are in there too. After all, it only takes two for church to be in session (Matthew 18:20).

Reach out to your mate. Someone once observed that happiness is being married to your best friend. If the home fires are cool it could be because somewhere along the way you stopped being your spouse's best friend. The hardest lesson that faced me during the first week of my marriage was that it wasn't going to be as easy as I had thought. After fifteen years, it still isn't easy. Merging two independent minds and spirits is never as simple as the romance novelists would have us believe. It takes work to build a relationship that will endure and satisfy.

Reach out to your children. I read somewhere that children are like comets. They shoot through our lives only to disappear into adulthood. Enjoy them now. Play with them. Hold them. Hug them. Love them before they slip into adulthood without ever really knowing you.

Reach out to others. Charity begins at home, but don't let it end there. Others need you too. We all lean on each other. We all support one another. Job 6:14 says, "For the despairing man there should be kindness from his friend; lest he forsake the fear of the Almighty." We all need someone to hold hands with.

SHARING WHAT WE HAVE RECEIVED

1975. It was a year of changes for me—and of depression. The first eight months were spent trying to minister in a place that didn't want me. The feeling was mutual. I didn't want some of them either. When no other options were open, we left. We moved back to Fort Worth so I could finish seminary.

I tried to work full time and take a full load at school. It didn't work out. I tried to find another place of ministry. That didn't work out. I tried to keep current on the bills. That didn't work out.

Then came the day my eighteen-month-old daughter wanted an apple. We had none. We had no way of getting any. We had just purchased a week's worth of groceries for our family of three-and-a-half in the express lane at the market.

I bottomed out.

Deborah drove off, intending to go home to her parents. A couple of hours later she returned and found me wallowing and rooting in a pig pen of self-pity.

I felt alone, alienated, betrayed by the God I thought I served. The words of my mom's friend came back, "You aren't saved. You never can be." I began to wonder again if she was right.

If God kept a hit list, I was sure I was on it. A step-child.

Worse, abandoned. A castaway. Not even worth recycling.

When the depression grew too great, I went to my pastor. I remember his words. "Larry, I don't understand depression. I never have. For me depression is occasionally feeling blue for an hour or two. I love you, but I can't help you."

I learned that day that the pain and suffering we bear is not ours alone. The darkness we endure, the loneliness, the rejection, the misfortune—all of it is for others as well. Our problems are destined to help us help others.

Do you know depression? Then you kow how to care for one depressed. Do you know despair? Then you know how to care for one despairing. Do you know grief? Then you know how to care for one grieving.

We are to comfort with the comfort with which we have been comforted. Whatever else that might mean, it also means that God expects us to use our darkness and His comfort to help others. As we have so needed a hug, we are to hug others.

How to Comfort

How does one comfort another? If we can just barely swim and another can't swim at all, how can we help him without both of us drowning?

Love them. Psychologists tell us that the three most important needs people have are to be loved, to feel important, and to feel secure. That means that one of the most valuable gifts we can give another is love—unconditional love. But love isn't always easy to give. How can we love someone who has hurt us? How can we love someone who turns us off? How can we love the unlovable?

C. S. Lewis gives us some insight in *The Voyage of the Dawn Treader.* Lucy was sent to find a spell for making hidden things visible. But in going through the magician's book of magic, she found another spell first—a spell that would let her know what her friends thought about her. Lucy spoke the words of the spell and found herself eavesdropping on two friends back in England:

> "Shall I see anything of you this term?" said Anne. "Or are you still going to be all taken up with Lucy Pevensie?"
>
> "Don't know what you mean by *taken up*," said Marjorie.
>
> "Oh yes, you do," said Anne. "You were crazy about her last term."

"No, I wasn't," said Marjorie. "I've got more sense than that. Not a bad little kid in her way. But I was getting pretty tired of her before the end of the term."

Lucy's response was immediate: "Well, you jolly well won't have the chance any other term! Two-faced little beast."[5]

Almost immediately Aslan, the Christ figure in the Narnian tales, confronted Lucy.

"Child," he said, "I think you have been eavesdropping."
"Eavesdropping?"
"You listened to what your two schoolfellows were saying about you."
"Oh that? I never though that was eavesdropping, Aslan. Wasn't it magic?"
"Spying on people by magic is the same as spying on them in any other way. And you have misjudged your friend. She is weak, but she loves you. She was afraid of the older girl and said what she does not mean."[6]

Lewis shows us there that no one loves us purely, nor we anyone else. We all are human. We all are weak and fearful. We all have warts. With God's grace I can overlook yours, and you can overlook mine.

Affirm them. According to William M. Kinnaird, affirmation brings out the best in people.[7] He's right. Everyone needs to be noticed and appreciated. When I am not appreciated, I not only feel diminished. I act diminished. But when I am valued, I blossom. I expand. I act value worthy. When I'm in a situation where I feel threatened, I clam up. I hide inside myself. When I feel accepted, I relax. I come out of my hiding place. Your acceptance of me helps me to accept myself.

Affirmation helps people grow. It does for most of us what heat does for sugared honey. Mark Twain said, "I can live for two months on a good compliment." I suspect most of us could say the same. Honest praise encourages us. It lifts us up. It may not give us the wings of eagles, but it will ease the load for the next several miles.

---

5. From *The Voyage of the Dawn Treader,*© C. S. Lewis, 1942, published by Collins. Used by permission.
6. Ibid.
7. Kinnaird, p. 55.

Create an attitude of hope. Charles Swindoll says,

> Our bodies have been constructed to withstand an enormous amount of pressure. God has made us to be fairly resilient people. We can survive the heat of the tropics or the icy winds of winter. With undaunted courage we can go through seasons of illness, financial reversals, domestic disappointments, unemployment or the death of someone dear to us... if we don't lose the one essential ingredient—hope.[8]

Hope is faith in seed form. It is the antidote to fear. Fear says, "I can't." Hope says, "Maybe I can." Hope inspires human Humpty Dumpties to look beyond all the king's horses and all the king's men unto the King himself. It whispers that the God whose mercy endures forever might also be a God who gives second, third, fifth, even hundredth chances.

Plant the seeds of a godly self-image. A godly self-image is seeing yourself through His eyes. The world hypes appearance and abilities. The beautiful and the talented, it claims, are happier, more successful, and better paid. In contrast the Bible says, "Man looks at the outward appearance, but the Lord looks at the heart" (2 Samuel 16:7).

Most of us aren't up to par on the beautiful and able scale. And according to Romans 3, none of us is up to par on the inner purity scale. Don't let that knowledge throw you.

Somehow, in spite of it all, God has loved, redeemed, adopted, and re-created us in Christ. That is good news for all of us.

Let them cry. Sometimes the best comfort we can give is a shoulder to cry on. Crying too often is viewed as a sign of weakness, immaturity, or inability to cope. We feel guilty, ashamed, silly for even wanting to cry. Crying runs contrary to some of the pop theology of our day. Christians, it suggests, are not supposed to cry. They're the winners, the overcomers. They're not supposed to have any more problems, any more sickness, any more pain.

The problem is that that view isn't scriptural. The Bible treats crying as normal and expected behavior in many situations. Abraham wept his grief over Sarah (Genesis 23:2). The mothers in Bethlehem wept for their sons slain by Herod (Matthew 2:18). Peter wept over his sin of denying Jesus

---

8. Charles R. Swindoll, "Hope," *Decision* (March 1985):6.

(Luke 22:62). Hannah wept her distress over her childlessness (1 Samuel 1:10). And Jesus wept for Lazarus (John 11:35).

Think about that. Jesus knew what had happened. And He knew what He was going to do. And He knew what would happen when He did it. Yet still He cried. He could have said, "Don't cry, Mary. It will be all right." But He didn't. He entered into her sorrow. And He showed His own.

Let others cry. Help them to overcome their discomfort. Accept their awkwardness. Treat it as a natural and acceptable thing. And let them find the relief that only crying can offer.

Let them talk. There is much inside them that needs to be verbalized. Like a steam valve on a pressure cooker, talking keeps them from exploding. Don't push them if they don't want to talk. The time will come on its own. But be available. And when it happens, be quiet and listen.

Don't play "If I were you, I'd . . ." games. There will be enough others around to offer unwanted advice. Too many are eager to emulate Job's friends. For our part, let's do the opposite. Where they discourage, let's encourage. Where they put down, let's lift up. Where they wearied Job with many words, let's listen with sympathy and care.

Face their problem yourself. Often we assume that we help them if we avoid mentioning their problem. We think that if we just carry on as usual things will be all right. That's false thinking.

Comfort is not assured by avoiding the issue but by facing it. The physician who helps us the most is the one who faces our sickness, not evades it. It's ridiculous to dodge talking about the pain of the one we seek to comfort. If someone has died, speak his name. Hearing it won't break a heart already bruised. It may even help it heal.

Allow them to reject your efforts. Comforting can't be force-fed. It can only be offered. Give grieving ones the right to reject it. Allow them to not do what we think or say. They may not be ready for the next step yet. They may not see things as we see them. They may not understand as we understand. They have the right to live by their own light—however clouded. Let's let them live with the same freedom we want to receive from others.

Give them time. It takes time to heal. It takes us time; it takes others time. Each one of us is different, with different recovery times. Let's remember that and give others the same right to time that we need. And let's not be content with one gesture of concern. Rather let's give sustained effort throughout their recovery.

10
BURNING BRIGHT BUT NOT OUT

Full circle.
We began in the water, over our head, going down for the third time. We began as a car four quarts low on oil. We began lost in a starless December midnight.

Step by step we learned how to tread water and how to float on our backs. We worked through undeserved tragedy, failure, and guilt. We learned what to do with unpleasant memories. We learned when to speak and when to listen. We discovered how to cultivate faithfulness and how to comfort as we've been comforted.

We are now in a position similar—but not identical—to where we were before our troubles began. We are stronger, more mature, but not yet full-grown. We've made some right decisions and some wrong decisions. We've endured ourselves back to shallow water. But our struggle for spiritual survival is not yet over.

One thing remains—learning how to burn bright but not out.

SPIRITUAL BURNOUT

John is a decent man, a loving husband and father. For

fifteen years he was active in his local church. But lately things have changed. He's dropped out of all the leadership positions he once held. In a year's time he's missed all but half a dozen services. He sends the wife and kids, if they want to go. But they've caught his attitude and usually don't. Now his Sundays are spent sleeping late, reading the paper, doing a few chores, and watching the tube.

A month ago, the last time John attended a service, his pastor spoke of Elijah lying under a juniper tree, complaining to God, and asking to die. John never realized that he and a biblical character could have so much in common. Something somewhere has soured in John's life. He feels tired, lonely, separated from God and from everyone else. He frowns constantly. And even trivial things seem more than he can handle. John is a victim of spiritual burnout.

Burnout is a colorful word. It brings to mind a number of images: the quenching of a rocket's red glare; light bulbs popping out in midair; the charred hulk of what once was a building; a power tool sputtering sparks and grinding to a halt. When applied to people, "the smell of psychological wiring on fire is everywhere."[1]

What is burnout? One answer is stress gone haywire. We all have stress—some good, some bad. Like fingers, toes, noses, and throats, stress is a basic part of being human. Without some stress we probably wouldn't function at all. Problems come when we have too little or too much. Too little stress leads to boredom. An overload of stress, inadequately handled, leads to burnout.

Burnout is the first and final hurdle to spiritual survival. Why the first? Because burnout often causes our being in the deep end in the first place. We tried and were disappointed—by ourselves, by others, by God. We found ourselves, in the words of one researcher, "in a state of fatigue or frustration brought about by devotion to a cause, way of life, or relationship that failed to produce the expected reward."[2]

We gave in to disappointment and cast ourselves into deeper water than we knew how to handle.

Why the last? Burnout is a little like the "go to jail" corner in Monopoly. Land on it and you go to jail without passing Go

1. Lance Morrow, "The Burnout of Almost Everyone," *Time* (21 September 1981):84.
2. Herbert J. Freudenberger and Geraldine Richelson, *Burn Out: The High Cost of High Achievement* (New York: Doubleday, 1980), p. 13.

and without collecting your $200. But skirt it, and you're in the final stretch for home. Give in to burnout, and you're tossed back into the ocean. Skirt it, and you're at least on dry ground.

The Causes of Burnout

Christians—especially those who've reached the point we're at now in this book—are particularly susceptible to burnout.

Why? Because, as someone observed, to have burnout you must first have a fire. The uncommitted and the uncaring may rust out or cop out. But they never generate enough heat to burn out. However, for someone who has just been through the valley or just come off the mountain top, the story is different. One has been in the crucible, the other touched by the burning bush. Both are aflame with the power of caring. They care about God. They care about others. They care about their relationship to Him and to them. And they care about how they ought to live in light of those relationships. True burnout is the exclusive property of someone who first cared.

One of the causes of burnout is unfulfilled expectations. We desire to make a difference for Christ in the lives of those around us. We want others to grow spiritually. We have a vision for other's betterment—and struggle to enflesh that vision. Yet when that vision fails to mesh with God's reality, when the desired results don't come, burnout crouches at the door.

The typical burnout began with high dreams. Sometimes the dreams were unrealistic, sometimes not. He worked long and hard but with few or no results. The frustration generated by the gulf between what he wanted to happen and what actually did happen turned inward. Soon the burning bush was scattered soot.

Another cause is overcommitment. Unfortunately we sometimes act as if we thought we came from the planet Krypton—super-Christians able to chair five committees, teach in Sunday school, witness, minister, and occasionally help with the offering, all in a single bound. We try to be spiritual men of steel, only to discover how frail we really are.

We are familiar with the workaholic and the high cost of his obsession. The religious version of that is the one who cannot say no. On the one side compulsion goads him, on the other legalism whips him, both pushing him to greater efforts.

And nowhere is the joy of serving to be found. He gives until there is nothing left to give and then fakes it as if he still had it.

In both unfulfilled expectation and overcommitment, uncontrolled disappointment is the match that gives flame to burnout. We expected one thing and received another. Disappointment sidled up and whispered, "Why? Why isn't God blessing your efforts? What's wrong with you? What's wrong with Him?"

Disappointment. It ate at Cain when Abel's sacrifice was accepted but his own wasn't. It festered in Job until he cursed the day he was born. It led the children of Israel to cry out against God at the Red Sea, in the wilderness of Sin, and at Meribah. It prompted Jonah to squat in anger, thirsting for Nineveh's destruction. The slide toward burnout begins with giving in to disappointment.

Then other factors contribute. A rocky relationship with God that leads to a rockier relationship that leads to a rockier relationship. A growing sense of futility and hopelessness. A negative self-image that says, "I don't belong; I don't meet the qualifications. I'm a hypocrite. God is better off without me." Armed with that fresh ammunition we spiral into the pits.

THE ELIJAH SYNDROME

That's what one researcher calls burnout—the Elijah Syndrome.

Elijah more than any other in the Bible shows all the classic symptoms of burnout. Burnout typically comes after walking through the valley of the shadow of death or after victory on the mountain top. For Elijah it was the latter. He confronted the prophets of Baal daringly and dangerously. He drank God's victory deep. Super-charged he outran Ahab's chariot down the mountain and back to Jezreel. Then abruptly, he was as burned out as the sacrifice he left behind on Mt. Carmel. (See 1 Kings 18-19.)

The burnout typically goes through three stages: (1) heating up—characterized by fuel shortage, fatigue, sleep disturbances, and escapist binges such as marathon television watching or shopping sprees; (2) boiling—characterized by constant anger, exhaustion, depression, and building to an almost incapacitating stew of pessimism, self-doubt, and obsession with one's own problems; and (3) explosion—characterized by apathy, a sense of hopelessness, and a desire to die.

Elijah arrived in Jezreel fuel short. He came off the mountain top spiritually as well as physically. The adrenaline was easing away, leaving fatigue and a vague sense of let down.

Immediately the prophet was greeted with Jezebel's vow to kill him before twenty-four hours had passed. That was the immediate catalyst for his burnout. He had just faced a more imminent death on Mt. Carmel had God not answered his prayer. But God had answered, and Elijah had won. Why should he run now?

What went through Elijah's mind as he outran Ahab to Jezreel? Did he expect a hero's welcome? Did he expect an immediate resurgence of belief in Yahweh that would drive Ahab and Jezebel from power—or at least curtail their pagan activities? He seemed to expect something other than what he received. What could move a man who had faced death several times over to suddenly flee, crying, "I alone am left"? What caused his mental horizon to close in and cut him off from any vision of God's workings? Only God knows.

We only know that depressed, discouraged, and alienated, Elijah arose in fear and ran for his life. He left his servant at Beersheba and went on a day's journey into the wilderness. In addition to being afraid, Elijah apparently longed just to be alone. The burnout often thinks that if he can just get away from everything and everyone, things will get better. It never works that way, though. On his own, cut off from any nurturing support of community, Elijah soon gave in to helplessness, emptiness, and despair.

There seemed nothing to live for. The victory was gone. The prophets of Baal were slain. But Jezebel would just invite new ones. He alone was left, and, considering Jezebel's past actions, he wouldn't be left for long. He didn't think much of himself right then: "I am not better than my fathers." The buildup and the boiling were complete. Elijah flopped under a juniper tree and asked to die.

An angel came and ministered to Elijah there. He awoke the prophet, gave him food and drink, then let him rest again. Later he reawoke Elijah, gave him more food and drink, and sent him on a forty-day hike to Mt. Horeb, where God had plans for dealing with the prophet.

The change of location didn't change Elijah's condition. When God asked the prophet what he was doing there, he vocalized his feelings of bitterness, loneliness, and persecution. "I have been very zealous for the Lord, the God of hosts;

for the sons of Israel have forsaken Thy covenant, torn down Thine altars and killed Thy prophets with the sword. And I alone am left; and they seek my life, to take it away" (1 Kings 19:10).

Elijah had been zealous. But his zeal had not brought what he sought. He felt self-important—and helpless. He alone was left. (What a blow it must have been to learn that God had 7,000 others who had not bowed to Baal.) And he felt paranoid. The "she" who had threatened him—Jezebel—became a "they"—the sons of Israel.

Moving into Maturity

Moving into maturity means learning to burn without being consumed. Loving, caring, striving to be the people God called us to be—these things were never meant to destroy us. They were to enrich our lives. They were to satisfy, fulfill, and attract. It is only when the control mechanism is damaged by discouragement that danger comes. Avoid that. Don't lose heart. Don't give in to discouragement. Instead reach for growth and maturity.

Someone has said that maturity isn't perfection but freedom—living freely but responsibly in the free grace of God. The word itself suggests "full grown" or "ripe." Obviously, we will never become totally mature. In a sense the only *ripe* Christian is the one who stands in the presence of God. He may not have been particularly ripe when he was plucked. But there he stands complete, changed, having traded in his old body for a new one unfettered by sin and decay. The impossibility of the goal, however, doesn't release us from trying.

Why should we try? Why should we grow?

Because when we stop growing—when we find a comfortable niche and hide in it—we open ourselves to stagnation and neurosis. Neurosis is a psychological term referring to unhealthy emotional quirks, usually involving anxiety, depression, and unresolved internal conflicts. These conflicts arise out of our personal insecurities, inferiority feelings, loneliness, pains, anger, lusts, and desires. They are normally not severe, just limiting. Psychologist Abraham H. Maslow defines neurosis as "failure of personal growth." He says, "All the evidence that we have indicates that it is reasonable to assume in practically every human being, and certainly in almost every newborn baby, that there is an active will toward health, an impulse toward growth, or toward the actualization of human potential. But at once we are confronted with the very saddening realization that so few people make it."[3]

How to Burn Bright, but Not Out

How can you make it? What can you do to be a lamp on a hill rather than a puddle of wax?

1. *Continue your spiritual education.* Most of us approach the spiritual life with shocking haphazardness. Turn that around. Begin now to plan moments of spiritual investment.

Start a personal survival seminar. You may be familiar with that under a different name: quiet time, devotional time, or Bible time. Don't let the familiarity of those names turn you off. You need regular contact with your Source.

Work particularly on attitude. Make this a time of spiritual hugs and loving one another, a time for renewing of relationship. Pray as you would talk to your closest friend, openly and honestly. Use your living language. God understands perfectly verbs that don't end in *est*, and He recognizes *yous* instead of *thees* and *thous*.

Your personal survival time doesn't need to be structured or lengthy. It does need to fit you, your schedule, and your needs. A few minutes a day is better than nothing. If particularly busy, you can pray—with your eyes open—as you drive to and from work or shopping.

2. *Realign your priorities.* We can never be overcommitted to Christ; but we can be overcommitted to programming. Learn to tell the difference. Too many irons in the fire means that none of the irons gets adequate attention. And it usually means that your family does without one of its most important parts—you. Fight overextension by realistically reappraising your priorities. What important things would God have you do? What are your abilities and limitations? What spiritual gifts have you been given? Learn how and when to say no. Your family will appreciate it even if some committee chairman doesn't.

3. *Relax.* Someone once quipped that rest sounded like something the devil invented just to keep believers from

---

3. Abraham H. Maslow, *The Farther Reaches of Human Nature* (New York: Viking, 1971), pp. 25-26.

doing God's work. Not so. Look at Jesus. As creator He worked six days, then took the seventh off. In His earthly ministry He seesawed between resting in the wilderness and ministering to people. When the twelve returned to Him after having been sent out in pairs, He said, "Come away by yourselves to a lonely place and rest awhile" (Mark 6:31).

Learn to slow down. Too often we act as if we were racehorses. We charge through our lives as if they were races to win. But "the race is not to the swift, and the battle is not to the warriors" (Ecclesiastes 9:11).

Psychologist Jerry R. Day recommends a simple relaxation technique. Take ten to twenty minutes at the end of the day to sit in a comfortable chair and enjoy a good stretch. Then starting with your toes, coax each part of your body to become warm, heavy, and relaxed. If it helps, you might imagine yourself basking on a warm tropical beach or strolling through a country meadow. Don't worry if at first you do not relax as much as you feel you should. Keep on doing it every day, and you will.

Another method of relaxing is to revive an old interest or hobby. Or start a new one. No one can make the fine handcrafted hardwood furniture you can make. No one can paint the picture you can paint or write the book you can write. Remember how much fun you had as a kid collecting this or that? Well, who said fun was just for kids? Read. Collect. Loaf. Enjoy yourself again.

4. *Exercise.* Almost all researchers agree that one of the best antibiotics for burnout is exercise. Take advantage of that? Walk, run, swim, play tennis, garden, golf. Do whatever interesting and enjoyable exercise you find that fits your temperament, schedule, and available resources.

5. *Laugh.* It isn't without reason that *Reader's Digest* entitles one of its joke sections "Laughter—The Best Medicine." It's true. Laughter has tremendous healing power. Laugh, not at the crudities and vulgarities of life, but in gentleness and wholeness. Learn to laugh at yourself. Oscar Wilde said, "People are never so trivial as when they take themselves very seriously." Seek out wholesome humor. W. H. Auden said, "Among those whom I like, I can find no common denominator; but among those whom I love, I can: all of them make me laugh."

6. *Seek community.* One writer has observed that "just as distancing, detachment, and withdrawal are allies of burnout,

so fellowship, closeness, and mutual edification are foes of burnout."[4] Don't try to be a spiritual Lone Ranger. Seek instead the mutual support of shared fellowship. Involve yourself with others.

The John Wayne mythos saturates our culture. We fantasize of lone heroes, capable, overcoming tragedy without support from anyone, standing tall, solitary, like a single powerful desert mesa. Our movies, television, and books focus on just such heroes. But real life works differently. We need each other. I need you. Together we can support each other. And together we can do things one man alone could never dream of.

Enrich your life at home. The family is God's primary support system. They love you. They care about you and need you to care about them. They need your special presence, your attention, your time, and generous doses of your love. Take time to enjoy them, play with them, hold them, hug them.

7. *Practice the art of thanksgiving and praise.* One researcher suggests that the best way to avoid burnout is to get "into the habit of noticing—and nurturing—the unspectacular good things that happen to us."[5] There is something about thanksgiving and praise that chases off disappointment like the sun does an early morning fog.

8. *Face your fears.* Someone has observed that "there is no one on this earth who is not twisted by fear and insecurity." Charlie Brown of "Peanuts" fame carried that thought a bit further and said, "I've developed a new philosophy. I dread only one day at a time."

Fear is almost always detrimental to your spiritual health. It is the great inhibitor, the great binder. Its icy grip drives flying from the heart and puts lead in the boots. It turns folks in on themselves, leaving them frustrated and unfulfilled.

Several years ago H. C. Brown wrote a little book entitled *Walking Toward Your Fears.* I like that title. Don't run from your fears. Face them. Walk toward them. Name them. Commit them to God. Turn loose of them. Let Him dispose of the garbage. Then refuse to retreat from what He has done.

9. *Refresh your spirit.* Relaxation and exercise refresh your

---

4. D. G. Kehl, "Burnout: The Risk of Reaching 'Too High,'" *Christianity Today* (20 November 1981):26-28.
5. Freudenberger, p. 199.

body. Find something to refresh your spirit. Discouragement makes us jaded. Like the man with the withered hand, we focus on our failures. We find ourselves locked into a cycle of doubt, depression, and disbelief. The antidote for this is faith, hope, and love. Zero in on the things that promote those. Go to a conference. Listen to a tape. Read a book. Examine the beauties of nature. Visit with a spiritual friend.

10. *Do the best you can for each day.* And refuse yourself the joy of worrying. Someone once defined worry as playing with tomorrow's garbage today. Stop it. Stop complaining to yourself about how miserable things are. Dwell on the good, not the bad. And remember, "if at first you don't succeed, you're running about average." When you foul up, take a deep breath and hit it again.

11. *Fight against feelings of alienation from God.* Try this exercise three times a day for a week. Imagine for a moment that you are a small child again. A big man walks in, picks you up, and hugs you. It's Jesus. He holds you close and whispers these words: "My child, I love you—good or bad, with no strings attached. And I accept you, just as you are. Don't try to change yourself; let Me do it when you're ready. I care about you. I care about everything that happens. And I forgive you—totally, completely, and forever."[6] Then He hugs you again and takes you out to play.

---

6. This exercise is adapted from Rosalind Rinker, *Communicating Love Through Prayer* (Old Tappan, N.J.: Revell, 1984). Used by permission.

11
GOING ON

God, are you really interested in me?
Well, I guess I know You are.
But out there in the deep water, I was scared. I thought I'd drown.
    And I was afraid of what might lie under the water.
    All my questions haven't been answered.
    At least I can tread water now. I can float on my back. And I can see the shore.
    With Your help, Lord, I think I'll make it. Shore is still a way off. But look how far You've brought me.
    Thank You, Lord.
    Oh, one other thing. Could You teach me to dog paddle now?

Moody Press, a ministry of the Moody Bible Institute,
is designed for education, evangelization, and edification.
If we may assist you in knowing more about Christ and the
Christian life, please write us without obligation:
Moody Press, c/o MLM, Chicago, Illinois 60610.